GOLF
How to become a champion

GOLF
How to become a champion

Nicholas Tremayne

William Luscombe Publisher Ltd
(In association with Mitchell Beazley Ltd)

First published in Great Britain by
William Luscombe Publisher Ltd.,
Artists House,
14–15 Manette Street,
London, W1V 5LB
1975

ISBN 0 86002 032 0

Filmset by Tradespools Limited, Frome, Somerset
Printed in Great Britain by Tinling (1973) Limited, Prescot

Contents

Illustrations

45 and 46 Casper demonstrating a pitch-and-run shot with a
    seven-iron. Note how the hands lead the clubhead into the
    ball   116, 117

*Both Author and Publisher wish to thank Mr Frank Gardner for permission to
reproduce his copyright photographs in this book*

Introduction

This is a book about champion golfers. Every member of the star cast has won at least one major international championship, and in most cases, several of the world's premier events. Collectively, their names read like a golfer's Who's Who of the modern era, and between them these thirteen players have won millions on the golf course.

To be a Champion is one thing, to be a great player, something else. Championships have been won out of the blue by a little-known golfer enjoying a golden week. Sometimes, as in the case of Lee Trevino and his victory in the 1968 US Open, such a win heralds the start of a wonderful career. More commonly, the overnight star sinks back into obscurity, and within a year or two, is forgotten. My definition of greatness is a player who achieves victory in a major championship, and then goes on proving that he can maintain that kind of form against the world's best opponents. Staying at the top has always been harder than reaching the top.

The players analysed in these pages have all either proved their greatness, or in my opinion, will do so over the next few years. They are all shapes and sizes, and have widely differing swings – yet they have all discovered the formula that keeps them at the top of the golfing tree.

There can be endless arguments about the relative strengths and weaknesses of different players, although few would argue that Nicklaus is the best driver in the world, Charles the best putter or Player the best at escaping from bunkers.

Where there is any possibility of argument I have chosen to recall great shots or great situations in major championships where this particular strength has been crucial. No doubt readers will disagree with some of my choices and recollect situations they witnessed, but I can only discuss events I have seen.

I hope those moments will bring back happy memories for a great many golfers who were privileged to be there.

NICHOLAS TREMAYNE

CHAPTER ONE

The Making of a Champion

Golf champions come in all shapes and sizes, from the diminutive Chi Chi Rodriguez – five-feet-seven and nine stones – to the gangling figure of George Archer, who stands a foot taller; from the pencil-slimness of Bob Charles to the cheerful rotundity of Bob Murphy.

Yet if these four golfers played against each other, no onlooker could predict with certainty the winner, nor could he maintain that any one method was more effective than another. He would see Rodriguez whiplashing the ball well ahead of the other three – he has consistently been one of America's longest hitters, despite his size; he would see Murphy conjuring the ball close to the hole with an almost magical wedge; and he would see Archer and Charles monotonously grinding out efficient shots one after another, before vying for the title of the world's best putter – one with a stiff-wristed stroke and the other with a wristy rap.

When learning the basic fundamentals of golf, the beginner is convinced that there is only one right way of playing the game. As likely as not he will believe that it is the method that his teacher is trying to instil in him, but after a while, when he has been beaten by golfers whose swings are quite different to the orthodoxy of his tutor, or perhaps when he has been to a professional tournament and seen the variety of swings which all seem to produce the same satisfactory result, he may change his opinion.

There is no 'right way' to play golf, simply because a number of variables are going to affect an individual's swing. Height, weight, age, suppleness, strength and temperament will combine to stamp their own mark on any golf swing. Yet, if there is any one 'secret' to successful golf it is something that Rodriguez, Archer, Murphy, Charles, and every other golfer we shall analyse in these pages has discovered: this is, the means of harnessing various swings in such a way that each is able to bring the clubhead squarely into the back of the ball at the maximum possible speed.

In other words, short and punchy, long and flowing, flat, or upright, no matter what the shape of the swing, all top golfers look exactly the same when the clubhead reaches the impact area.

Fashion and fad have played important parts in golf techniques, just as in more or less every other area of our lives. With the emergence of Tom Weiskopf and Johnny Miller into the super-star class, would-be champions have supreme examples of classic, flowing swingers to study. They are good models to emulate, for they manage to combine the standard teaching principles and basic doctrines of sound golf.

But when Palmer was at the height of his powers there were club golfers all over the world exhibiting the 'blocked' follow-through which is so characteristic of his swing. When Jack Nicklaus asserted himself as the world's best golfer, his upright backswing and flying right elbow were studied closely from action photographs and soon became familiar features of so many Sunday morning fourballs.

Copyists had often forgotten the most important fundamental of the game – it does not matter how you arrive there, as long as the clubhead is travelling straight along the target-line at maximum speed for a foot or so on either side of the ball. They did not relate Palmer's follow-through position with the position of his left wrist at the top of the backswing; nor did they relate Nicklaus's height, posture at address and the strength of his legs to his upright action. All they were doing was caricaturing idiosyncracies in the masters' swings in the mistaken belief that Palmer and Nicklaus had discovered a new way of playing golf, and that the secret they were refusing to impart was the key to fame and fortune.

The good golf teacher can only pass on to pupils a few basic and well-tried principles. He does not expect that every product of his teaching will swing the club in the same way; he knows that the complex inter-relationship of physical and mental factors will shape their own individuality into every golf swing. Sometimes he is compelled to work within certain constraints – age, stiff joints, physical defects – and then he must help to develop a swing which still enables the player to conform to that basic square/velocity principle.

Among the champions of today there is an outstanding example of this. As a boy, Gay Brewer damaged his right elbow in a football accident and because the joint would not allow his right arm to fold naturally on the backswing, he developed a curious figure-of-eight loop far from the stylist's ideal. It has not, however, prevented him from winning an American Masters title, over $600,000 in his own country and perhaps another £100,000 in different parts of the world.

The first common essential of all champions: the golf swing is merely a vehicle for hitting a small white ball straight and far. It does not matter that for nine-tenths of their swings they all look different. What does concern them is that during that vital one-tenth, they should all be doing the same thing.

The second essential is even more nebulous. Temperament. Mental outlook separates a man from his fellows even more than physical characteristics. There are perhaps a thousand golfers in the world today with the shot-making ability to become outstanding international champions. If they are lucky, perhaps half a dozen will make it. Go to any tournament and you will see little to choose between the vast majority of competitors. Go to a major championship, and you immediately feel the wide gulf between the elite few from whom you expect the winner to emerge, and the others who are there, a little sadly, to make up numbers.

A difference of attitude, bearing and confidence sets champions apart. The aspiring tournament star may say, with some justification, that it is easy to have the right attitude to winning when you have already won often enough to make it a habit; when you are established, when the publicity machine looks upon you as a winner. Indeed, success does help breed success, but what is so often forgotten is that there has to be a successful launching pad – that first victory from which everything else follows. That first victory, more than any other, requires the mental stamina on which every champion relies.

There are few fairy-tales in modern professional sport, but the story of Lee Trevino is worth recounting for the insight it gives into his attitude. In 1967 at the age of 28, Trevino was an almost destitute driving-range professional in El Paso, Texas, supplementing his meagre income by hustling for a few dollars on the local golf courses. His wife sent the entry form and $20 fee to the United States Golf Association, organizers of the US Open Championship.

Little attention was paid to the swarthy, stocky Mexican who arrived at Baltusrol via the local qualifying event to take his place on the first tee at one of the world's greatest events. With the classic situation of Nicklaus fighting out the finish with Palmer, few eyebrows were raised, few people noticed, that this unknown with a flat, raking swing had finished fifth.

It was not, after all, unheard-of for unknown club pros to feature strongly in the Open. But for Trevino, it was the most important day of his life. He had come to New Jersey for a week's holiday, and now found himself with a cheque for $6,000 – more money than he had ever handled before. There the story might have ended, with Trevino fading back into Texan obscurity, but his wife encouraged him to use the money to play in a few more tournaments, and by the end of the year he had added another $20,000 to his bankroll.

The 1968 US Open was played at Rochester, New York. Again Jack Nicklaus was the centre of attraction, and again he was fighting out the finish. But this time there was a swarthy, stocky Mexican in front of him. Trevino, showing no signs of humanity or frailty, forged unassailable rounds of 69, 68, 69, 69 to win by four strokes from Nicklaus. He had picked what is arguably the world's most difficult tournament to record his first victory.

Winning a major championship does not necessarily make a superstar. In 1969, Orville Moody relieved Trevino of his title – and then sank almost without trace. As we now know, Trevino's week at Rochester was merely the springboard for one of golf's most startling and effervescent careers. Three years later, he was to win the American title again – in a play-off with Nicklaus – the Canadian Open, and then journey to Royal Birkdale to win the British Open . . . and all within the space of three weeks. He was successfully to defend his Open Championship at Muirfield in 1972, and was unquestionably to stand alongside Nicklaus and Gary Player as one of the world's outstanding champions. And all from $20 his wife sent to the USGA . . .

Of course, there was a lot more to it than the wheel of fortune and a cheque for $20. Trevino had ability, he had courage; from his experience of gambling for more money than he could ever afford to lose, he had built his own armour against pressure. And having made that first great breakthrough, he set about making himself into a personality that the publicity machine would never be able to forget. Who knows whether in June 1968, Trevino was able to foresee such an incredible and meteoric career? But having created an image that nobody could afford to ignore, he must psychologically have felt that he was a great champion.

Is there a common temperamental ingredient that the champions possess and that other mortals do not? Is it possible to compare the ebullient, clowning personality of Trevino with the dour isolation of Bruce Crampton? One sees himself as a public entertainer and the other as a professional golfer who lives only by the quality of his game.

On the surface, there is no basis for comparison between these widely divergent characters. Nevertheless, underlying their attitudes to the game they both love, there is a common bond – the quality of single-mindedness.

Shortly after his triumph at Rochester, Trevino told me: 'People think I'm a funny guy, a happy guy who doesn't give a damn about anything. I remember what it was like for me as a kid, I remember what it was like only a couple of years ago. I never want to see that kind of life again. I guess that no matter how successful I may be, no matter how much money I'm able to invest, I shall never be able to forget those days . . . and I shall always be just a little afraid.'

Analysing motives which individuals may not even have analysed for themselves is a difficult and dangerous thing to do. Perhaps from studying their characters one can get an inkling of what motivates the great champions. Trevino saw golf as the only means by which an underprivileged Mexican could achieve fame and fortune. Palmer loved the game, and still does, for the competition; he is past the imperious peaks he set in the 1950s and early 1960s, perhaps the chance of one more major title has gone for ever. Still he competes, and still a tournament victory means more to him than another million dollars. At one stage, Nicklaus so dominated the world of golf that the competitive element was largely removed. He had only to enter a tournament and the psychological effect of his presence automatically gave him a better than even chance of victory. So he set about re-writing the pages of history by winning more of the world's major championships than any other man. Gary Player simply wanted to prove that his size need not be a barrier to him becoming the world's best player.

Whatever their motivations, and the motivations of men like Billy Casper, Bob Charles, Ben Hogan, Tony Jacklin, Johnny Miller and Tom Weiskopf, their efforts have been channelled into a single-mindedness that would have made them successful in almost any profession or business. Golf is a distillation of concentration, dedication and imagination.

No matter how outward personalities may conceal the rigidity of determination, it is always the most important single characteristic of any champion in any sport.

A vital difference between 'them' and 'us' is in their use of imagination. For most club golfers, imagination runs only as far as a mental picture of stepping up and receiving the silver cup from the club Captain, and the opening lines of the speech of thanks. Unfortunately, this image usually assails the mind somewhere around the 16th when the player is in with a good chance. The pattern is familiar; concentration wanders, the player slices into the trees, panics . . . And suddenly that rosy picture fades away.

The champion puts his imagination to work in a more practical and ordered way. Even before he steps on to the first tee, his mind is creating a mental image of the shot he is about to play. He knows the shape of the hole, he knows that the approach to the green is best made from the left side of the fairway, and so he pictures the flight of the ball and the swing he must make in order to produce that flight. When he walks up to the second shot, he is already going through the same routine.

As anyone who has played competitive golf knows only too well, the most difficult thing is to concentrate on one shot at a time. Yet this is the most often repeated piece of advice that tournament professionals give to amateur golfers. Different people mean different things by 'concentrate', and a great many will think only in terms of technique, on trying to execute a technically perfect swing. When one is in a pressure situation, this is almost impossible, and in fact, analysis of function can so easily lead to paralysis of execution.

A grooved golf swing is not only the prerogative of the champion golfer; even the middle-handicap player (if he plays regularly) has a grooved swing. True, his swing will not be as technically efficient as the top tournament star's, certainly he will have his limitations. But when playing in a competition all he can ask of his method is that it works as well as it can within those admitted limitations. So when he concentrates on a particular shot, is it not best for the club golfer to picture the best shot that his limitations will allow?

It is strange how such a positive image actually works on the muscles and encourages them to produce a swing that produces a flight and shape that successfully carbon-copies the mind's-eye picture. The theories of mind over matter, of psyche over physiology, demand a positive attitude or belief. A clear mental picture of the shot to be played, discounting the potential dangers and eliminating thoughts of failure, is simply a method of psyching oneself into the best possible frame of mind for producing the best possible shot.

The champion golfer, of course, is at a distinct advantage. One of the prerequisites of being a champion is that he has absolute confidence in his ability as a shot-maker. It is confidence borne of past experience and the labour of many hours on the practice ground. When he is playing a crucial shot at a vital stage of a major championship, he is concentrating on blocking out intrusive fears so that his experienced muscles will be allowed to produce their natural swing from habit. What the club golfer has to remember on monthly medal day is that his muscles, too, have a memory of their own and that left to their own devices they will produce their familiar swing. The handicap golfer is unlikely ever to have the ability of a champion, nor would he aspire to such heights. But if he only learned to think like a champion, to develop a champion's imagination and to use it in this practical way as the power of concentration, he would be bound to improve his golf beyond recognition.

Champions are sufficiently dedicated to actual practice that they work at their games harder than most. A real champion is a man who can maintain his success once he has become a super-star. The pressure is even greater when you know that every other competitor in the field is gunning for you.

There are times, of course, when every golfer's swing slips out of its groove and needs a technical overhaul. But the hours the champions spend hitting balls is generally time spent in trying to perfect their rhythm. The tempo of the swing is such an individual thing that it can only be built into the action through such long and lonely hours.

The beginner is always told to swing the club slowly. As he becomes more experienced, he appreciates that the speed of swing varies enormously from player to player. Generally, the slow-moving, methodical man tends to swing the club lazily, while the quick and nimble personality produces a much faster swing.

What every player must strive for is a swing that is a smooth entity, with one phase flowing evenly into another. Because we learn to swing the club through three distinct phases – backswing, downswing and follow-through – there is a distinct danger of mentally breaking the entire action down into three separate units, forgetting that only by keeping it in one continuous and smooth arc can we develop maximum clubhead velocity.

Most tournament players believe that competition each week is sufficient to keep their games sharp, and only settle down to prolonged practice sessions when things start to go awry. The great champions, however, work hardest on their games when they are playing their best. They know that they are practising a good swing and a good rhythm, and that by ingraining that action in their subconscious they are giving themselves the best possible chance of maintaining peak form for as long as possible.

Happy-go-lucky Trevino may appear to be, but when he is away from the public eye, he practises as hard as anyone. Gary Player has almost made a fetish of practice. This occasioned one of the game's great throw-away lines. Playing in a tournament, the little South African holed out from a greenside bunker. When, in a muttered undertone, a member of the gallery suggested to those in his immediate vicinity that Player had been more than a little fortunate, Gary strolled across the green and remarked: 'Yes, funny that. The more I practise, the luckier I get.'

What is extraordinarily impressive about the world's great players is their ability to bring themselves to a peak of sharpness at exactly the right moment. Trevino, Weiskopf or Miller, while having a psychological advantage at a run-of-the-mill tournament, may not necessarily play at a different level to the majority of their fellow-competitors. But when they arrive at the venue of an Open Championship they quite automatically become part of the elite band that the crowds are going to watch. Their preparation is at a peak; on the practice ground and in practice rounds on the golf course they have brought themselves to the ultimate pitch of readiness.

Most of the super-stars have appreciated that they can only play so much of their best golf in any one year. Nicklaus, in particular, strictly limits his number of tournament appearances by taking regular breaks from the gruelling circuit of the world's golf courses. He goes fishing, or follows one of his many business interests, or just stays home with the family for a few days. He has planned his campaign at the beginning of the year, so he knows when it is time to head for the practice ground to begin his preparations for the next target. Perhaps players of his calibre are at an advantage because they are so financially secure they can aim only at the prestige events, without having the weekly scramble at the Mini-Mornington Open in order to pay the grocery bills.

The club golfer does not want to put in hours of practice; his time at the club is short and very precious. He needs the camaraderie of his friends, the cut-and-thrust of the Sunday fourball, and a few drinks in the bar to refresh him from the labours of the office routine. If he is really anxious to improve, however, he might bear in mind that ten minutes' thoughtful and constructive practice is worth more than aimlessly hitting balls for hours. Practice for its own sake is tedious and can be destructive if boredom makes you careless. Practice with a purpose, if only for a few minutes, gives the time and opportunity to make a true analysis of the swing and its problems.

Not so long ago, golf was damned as an 'old man's game'. The grind of the American pro circuit, and these days the European circuit as well, which continually drain a man's physical and mental resources, has given the lie to that old adage. Physical fitness is now a priority both with the champions and the also-rans of professional and top amateur golf. They watch their weight, they watch their diet, and they watch their drinking, just as any other athlete would.

Obviously, physical fitness is not so important for the weekend golfer, but equally obvious, the fitter he is the better he will perform, and the more he will enjoy his game. There are times when fitness counts, as when one plays extra holes in the club's knockout competition, or when playing in a 36-hole event.

Nobody who plays golf for fun is going to make a task of the game. Yet, in a sport we all know cannot be completely mastered, we will all derive most fun when we are playing as well as we are capable.

These then are the common characteristics of all champions: they all hit the ball fast and square, albeit with a variety of swings; they all possess single-mindedness, having learnt to put imagination to practical work; all are dedicated to practice; all are aware of the single most important feature of the swing – rhythm; and all are physically fit.

Those ingredients can be absorbed by the handicap golfer, and if he keeps them in mind, he is bound to improve his game immeasurably without making any technical changes to his swing.

The seventh characteristic of the champions which divorces them from the rest of us is their supreme shot-making ability. Even the greatest players will hit a proportion of bad shots – a comforting factor to most spectators when they witness a real hacker's shot at a major tournament. But in order to remain champions they are good in every department of the game, and usually superb in one or two departments. Around these areas of their greatest strengths they build their entire game.

So let us see what we can learn from studying the world's best players in their particular areas of strength.

CHAPTER TWO

The Champion Driver: Jack Nicklaus

Power, so they say, corrupts. To the extent that improved equipment has helped the top professionals to hit the ball further and further from the tee – and this factor has had a direct bearing on the design of new golf courses – this is partially true.

Seemingly, golf course architects are increasingly designing courses with the professional and the top-class amateur in mind, forgetting that club golfers who play regularly over the course do not possess the power to cope with excessive length. Club committees, too, must bear some of the responsibility. If they want a new course built they say it must be of 'championship standard', by which they really mean 'championship' length. Since the par of courses has been directly related to length, many committees have insisted on building new tees and lengthening holes merely to get another shot or two added to the Standard Scratch Score.

If carbon-fibre ever becomes widely accepted among the professionals as the best material for a driver shaft because it can give them another 20 or 30 yards on their tee shots, heaven knows where it will all end. Already no new golf course design coming off the drawing board is worth its salt unless the minimum is 7,000 yards. How soon can we expect 8,000 yards as the norm?

In these times of soaring land prices and increased pressure on the use of land, few countries in the world will keep pace with the game's growth by supplying enough golf courses unless this idiocy stops.

Golf's ruling bodies have been discussing the possibilities of limiting the velocity of the modern golf ball in order to control power. Who knows? perhaps they have also considered banning steel shafts and compelling a return to hickory. Such thinking, surely, is approaching the problem the wrong way round. When you and I, who comprise 99·99 per cent of golfers, feel that we do not have the power to cope with existing golf courses, why should our limitations be even more exposed by an artificial restriction on equipment - we need the best gear technologists can produce!

I submit that it is the golf courses themselves that the game's fathers should be looking at. If they could encourage architects to build shorter, narrower and more subtle layouts, this alone would be sufficient to curb the power of the top professionals. No man playing for his living is going to reach automatically for his driver at a narrow, tree-lined, well-bunkered 400-yard hole. He is going to rely on the accuracy of a long iron from the tee to keep him on the fairway, and

1   A heavyweight Nicklaus pictured in the 1960s in a purposeful and solid address position. Notice the interlocking grip

2   The modern Nicklaus, slimmer and trendier, but still hitting the ball just as far from the tee. Here is the perfect example of the 'sitting-down' position, and the flying right elbow is very apparent

then he plays a longer second shot to the green.

Ask Jack Nicklaus, not only the world's best golfer but also consistently the most powerful, which course he considers the most demanding championship test, and he will nominate a relatively old-fashioned course in Pennsylvania measuring a mere 6,500 yards. Nicklaus has good cause to remember Merion because he is only one of two men to have attained a four-round par of 280 in three US Open Championships. Unfortunately for him, the other was Trevino who did it in the same week, and then beat him in a play-off the following day for the 1971 American Open. Even Hogan at the height of his powers could do no better than 287 when he won at Merion in 1950, and Olin Dutra's total in 1934 was 293.

For the top professionals, length is quite incidental; there is certainly no contest between them. Gary Player, at his best, can compete on level terms against Nicklaus, despite the fact that Big Jack has a potential advantage of 60 yards or more from the tee. What Player lacks in length at this highest level of the game, he makes up for with accurate iron play and superb touch round the greens.

Nevertheless, power from the tee holds a special fascination for the club golfer. He feels, wrongly, that length is the factor that separates him most from the professionals, and that if only he could hit the ball a bit further, nobody in his club could beat him.

When Nicklaus heads for the practice ground at an Open Championship, he takes the inevitable army of spectators with him. His warm-up routine is the same as any other professional's, he starts by hitting little pitch shots, then gradually works up through the bag hitting the driver last of all. It is very noticeable how little attention the spectators pay to the way he plays the finesse and precision shots. They reserve their oohs and ahs and unbutton their camera cases for the moment when he reaches for the driver.

Nicklaus is the best player in the world because he has few peers in any department of the game, although one wonders how many more of the great championships he might have won if he had been blessed with Bob Charles' or Gary Player's putting ability from eight feet and under.

But perhaps it is true to say that his immensely accurate driving was the cornerstone on which the rest of his game was developed. Any champion has to be an outstanding short-iron player if he is going to squeeze every possible birdie out of the course, and Nicklaus's capacity for reducing so many holes to drives and short pitches has brought its rewards.

Indeed, it was just such a situation that produced one of the most electrifying and crucial shots seen in Britain for many years. The 18th at St Andrews, where the 1970 Open Championship was played, is a relatively innocuous hole. There are broad acres to drive into, and the out-of-bounds wall on the right will worry only the wildest slice. What problems the hole possesses are concentrated around the green, for just short of the putting surface is the deep hollow known as the Valley of Sin which can turn the pitch shot into a battle of nerves; the green itself is full of intimidating slopes.

In the cool of that July Saturday evening in 1970, this hole was the centre of one of the saddest dramas in Open Championship history. The colourful and popular Doug Sanders, one of the Open's greatest supporters, needed a par four to win the title. All too aware of the lurking dangers of the Valley of Sin, he played his pitch shot boldly to the back of the green, nine yards past the flag. He left the downhill putt a yard or so short, and then after much shuffling and hesitation, watched his second putt slide away to the right of the hole.

And so into a play-off against Nicklaus the following day. It was a battle that Big Jack dominated most of the way, but over the closing holes, Sanders fought back bravely and finally came to the 18th only a stroke in arrears. His drive at this 358-yard hole was straight and true, leaving him an orthodox pitch-and-run shot over the Valley of Sin. He was in a good position to make a birdie.

Now Nicklaus was forced to do something special. To maintain his advantage he had to make a birdie, and the easiest way of doing that was by driving the green. Stripping off his sweater, Nicklaus launched into the ball, and to thunderous applause watched as it pitched on to the front of the green, ran up the entire length of the putting surface, and trickled into the short rough at the back. He had hit a drive of over 380 yards, but more incredibly, had *pitched* it 335 yards in order to carry the Valley of Sin.

Sanders is not a man to give up easily. His pitch-and-run shot left him a five-footer for his birdie, and now once again the pressure was on Nicklaus. His chip shot down the green was a little tentative, and left him a similar putt to the one Sanders had missed the previous evening, but three times as long. With the adrenalin still flowing from his mighty drive, in the ball went, and this time Sanders made no mistake, so the play-off margin was a single shot. But if ever a drive won an Open Championship, it was this stunning blow from Nicklaus.

The Nicklaus Method
Power for its own sake is of no value to a top-class player; but controlled power, as we have seen in this example, can win championships. Jack Nicklaus is enormously strong physically, but the important thing to remember is that much of his strength is used in *controlling* the build-up of power in his swing, rather than directly creating that power.

A simple principle of physics tells us that an object attached to the end of a rod, which in turn is attached to a fixed axis, will move faster through an arc the further it is from the axis. This is the key to Nicklaus's length from the tee: his golf swing is designed to put the clubhead on the widest possible arc so that he can create maximum clubhead velocity with the minimum physical work-effort.

When he first appeared as a professional in 1961, some critics suggested that his swing could be unreliable. They studied particularly the way in which he allowed his right upper-arm to leave the side of his body on the backswing, and the term 'flying right elbow' became commonly used. This action went completely against the traditional teaching concepts, when pupils were told that they should be able to hold a handkerchief under the right arm throughout the backswing.

Fortunately, times have changed and teachers realize now that a wide arc cannot be created unless the upper-arm is allowed to drift away from the body. Less than twenty years ago we were taught that accuracy was the most vital component of a golf shot. It has taken players of the calibre of Palmer and Nicklaus to admit that as youngsters they learnt to hit the ball hard, and thoroughly enjoyed it, before building accuracy and control into their swings.

Like most very long hitters, Nicklaus's swing can be broken down into three important areas – the speed and flexibility of his leg action, the degree of shoulder turn and the strength of his hands. The first two features are mainly responsible for the width of his arc, the third – hand action – is what provides him with control.

3   Through the ball, the right leg provides tremendous momentum, and the long right arm is driving towards the target

The grip
Nicklaus makes a slight alteration to the standard overlapping, or Vardon, grip that is widely accepted as the most comfortable and efficient for the mass of golfers. Instead of overlapping the left forefinger with the little finger of the right hand, he interlocks these two fingers. He maintains that this helps him to weld the two hands into one cohesive unit. He is not the first top golfer to make this adjustment – Dai Rees also uses an interlocking grip – and as long as the basic principle of proportionate opposition of the two hands is not upset, the use of this grip is a matter of simple preference.

Indeed, handicap golfers who find themselves letting go at the top of the backswing may feel that the interlocking grip is more secure, although wrist action is very slightly limited.

The grip really is the most fundamental of all the principles we learn in golf. The positioning of the hands on the club can affect the shape and arc of the swing, and it is only through the hands that the build-up of power is ultimately transmitted to the clubhead. Apart from his preference for an interlock, Nicklaus's grip is absolutely orthodox, as are the grips of all the other champions we shall be studying in these pages. They have learnt that there is no substitute for a sound and conventional grip on the club. Apparently, a great many club golfers do not believe this, judging by the assortment of odd grips one can see at any golf club on a Sunday morning. Age and physique is no bar to developing a good grip. All that is required is a little effort to accustom oneself to the feel, and constant vigilance to check that the hands are not slipping into a bad position. Even when the grip is second nature, it is all too easy to slide into bad habits without realizing. The champions check the position of their hands on the club constantly: so should you.

Stance: The most noticeable feature of Nicklaus's set-up position with a driver is that he gives himself a wide base on which to operate. Most professionals recommend that their pupils should stand with their feet at the same width, or only slightly wider, than the width of the shoulders.

Because Nicklaus has one of the biggest body turns in the game, combined with a fast and powerful leg action, his wider-than-average stance does not restrict the fullness of his swing. His stance is slightly open, so that he is more likely to fade the ball from the tee than play with draw.

The ball is positioned well forward in the feet, opposite the left instep, and once he is set up, the left arm and shaft of the driver form one straight line. By having hands and clubhead so well forward, his right shoulder is considerably lower than the left.

There is no tension in his powerhouse legs, and any bending forward is from the waist, keeping the back fairly straight.

Backswing: Nicklaus's takeaway is a model for all to study. This vital first stage of the swing, that sets the pattern for the rest of the movement, is the most important – yet most overlooked – area of the golf swing. It is also one of the simplest movements to achieve correctly.

Nicklaus starts the club back with the classic one-piece movement – arms, hands and clubhead all moving as one solid unit without the wrists breaking. By taking the club straight back from the ball, low to the ground, he is initially creating the widest, and therefore most powerful, swing.

Because he maintains this one-piece action for as long as possible (until the hands are well above hip height) his swing automatically becomes upright – with the hands very high at the top. Only by allowing his left leg the freedom to break in towards the ball does he release the top half of his body so that the shoulders complete one of the biggest turns in golf. The one-piece takeaway starts the club on a wide arc, the free leg action and big turn maintains that width.

Most golfers have learnt from the outset that accuracy is more important than power, and that one of the greatest sins they can commit is to sway on the backswing. This inherent fear of swaying is one of the most constraining influences in the club golfer's swing. Only when he allows the legs to unlock and the shoulders to make a full turn is he going to follow Nicklaus's example of a wide arc.

Another point that seems to worry a great many handicap players is the position of the left wrist at the top of the swing. This is something that no golfer should ever worry about, since it merely reflects the positioning of the hands on the club and the shape of the backswing. In Nicklaus's case, the upright arc of the swing dictates that the left wrist is very slightly concave at the top. Arnold Palmer's flatter swing produces a position where the left wrist and forearm form a straight line. But it is important to remember that the position achieved is an effect and not a cause. If the club golfer finds that his wrist position changes, then he should look for the cause in his grip, because almost certainly some subtle alteration in the hand positioning is responsible.

Downswing: It is coming down into, and through, the impact area where one really appreciates the two contra-forces of Nicklaus's swing with a driver.

First, there is the tremendously powerful forward thrust supplied by the legs; then there is the firm left hand and arm which channels and controls forward momentum. Mathematicians and physicists will prove that maximum force is produced only when there is an element of resistance to the motor. In Nicklaus's case, that resistance is represented by his entire left side, which remains firm without inhibiting the freedom of the action in any way.

Golf teachers used to talk of 'hitting against a braced left side', and action photographs of the pre-war professionals show them at impact with ramrod-straight left legs. In order to achieve this position they were compelled to unwind the hips on the downswing with a very fast rotating motion. Not only was this a difficult movement to time exactly, but it also led to the danger that the right shoulder would be thrown forward and the plane of the swing made out-to-in across the ball.

Today's top golfers never think in terms of a 'braced' left side, but of a *firm* left side – for the modern power method has successfully combined firmness with fluidity . . . and incidentally, very largely removed the danger of hip injuries that the pre-war method was always likely to cause.

As Nicklaus demonstrates so well, the function of the hips is to initiate the downswing, at the same time keeping the clubhead on the inside plane. Also, by combining his hip and leg movements, he is able to hit right through the ball, producing the long right arm extension towards the target which sets the champions apart from the rest of us.

It is the hips that start the downswing by sliding forward laterally, and at the same time beginning to unwind. This action alone is sufficient to bring Nicklaus's hands down to hip-height, in a late-hitting position, without any conscious movement of the arms or shoulders. Thus, he has immediately put the plane of the swing on to an inside-to-out arc, and given the right shoulder no chance to float forward – perhaps the most oft-committed of sins among club golfers when they have a big club in their hands.

Only when the hands are at hip-height, and the left hand and arm have started pulling the clubhead in towards the ball, does the right shoulder begin to move – and then the movement is down and *under* the chin, not round.

The initial hip movement has also begun the vital process of weight transference from the right leg to the left. The two movements are so inextricably linked that Nicklaus does not have to make any conscious effort to transfer the weight through the ball. If the forward hip-slide is timed in its proper sequence, the weight will move as a natural consequence. But one can appreciate just how impossible this action would be if the left leg had remained stiff. The knee acts as a kind of shock absorber, and 'gives' a little without ever becoming sloppy.

In the impact area, particularly, there is a strong impression that the entire left side of Nicklaus's body is acting almost like a brick wall. His head is well behind his left leg, which is absorbing the entire forward thrust of the swing, and his left hip is not permitted to move forward any further once clubhead and ball have made contact. Here is the resistance that maximizes power.

The left hand and arm are the controlling influences in the impact area. From the time his hands have reached the right hip on the downswing, to the moment they pass the left hip on the through-swing, the left arm remains straight and firm. It is the spoke in the wheel that keeps the arc of the swing constant round the axis of his head.

It is the left hand that directs the clubhead into the back of the ball, allowing the right hand and arm to unleash their pent-up power at the critical moment – a piece of timing that takes place quite naturally. Once contact has been made, it is the right hand that dominates by driving the clubhead on towards the target, but even at this point, Nicklaus does not allow the left arm to be totally over-ridden. If the left arm is allowed to collapse too soon, the long right

4   *Jack Nicklaus is enormously strong physically, but the important thing to remember is that much of his strength is used in* controlling *the build-up of power in his swing, rather than directly creating that power*

arm extension through the ball will be completely dissipated, and instead of the clubhead following the target-line, it will drag to the left of that line.

Follow-through: Leslie King, one of Britain's most respected golf teachers, often starts by perfecting the follow-through of a new pupil before considering backswing and downswing. He maintains that a good follow-through can only be developed if the preceding movements are correct.

Nicklaus possesses a classic end-of-swing position, with his balance perfectly maintained. Immediately after impact his left leg straightens in readiness to bear almost his full weight. The right arm continues to drive through the ball perfectly straight, and remains that way until his hands have passed eye-level. But the rotating of his hips towards the target, so that his belt-buckle is pointing straight down the fairway, has taken him comfortably into the perfect position, with his hands high at the finish.

The most important thing to notice about his finish to the swing is that his head, which was planted securely behind the invisible 'wall' of his firm left side, has remained in that exact position, even though it has rotated so that his eyes are now following the flight of the drive. He has not allowed his head to move forward with the force of this immensely powerful swing, and if ever a club golfer needed a model to understand the most repeated piece of golfing advice – 'keep your head *still*' – he could do no better than to watch Jack Nicklaus.

CHAPTER THREE

The Fairway Woods: Sam Snead

It would be true to say that among today's champions there is no champion fairway wood player. A startling statement perhaps, particularly when we like to believe our heroes are invincible.

Of course, there have been some great and crucial wooden shots hit. Arnold Palmer's magnificent three-wood into the teeth of the wind at Royal Birkdale's 18th hole during the 1965 Ryder Cup is a shot that lives in my memory. It was the afternoon of the final day with the Americans setting the seal on their victory in the second series of singles. Palmer, playing top for America, had been unable to shake off the dogged attentions of Peter Butler, and came to the par five 18th one up. For ordinary mortals, the green was out of range, but Palmer wound himself up and let fly with everything his considerable physique possesses. Standing behind the green, I watched the flight of the ball all the way – beading straight at the flag, and never more than twenty feet from the ground. It finished four feet away to give Palmer an eagle, and a two-hole victory.

Then there was Neil Coles's four-wood to the 18th green at Troon. The 1973 Open had been a two-man affair, the only doubt being whether Johnny Miller could finally overtake Tom Weiskopf. But in the freshening breeze of the last day, Neil Coles was placidly compiling one of the rounds of the championship. A four into the wind at the last would give him a 67. He did better than that. His four-wood settled ten feet from the hole, and in went the putt to give him a total of 279 and a tie for second place with Miller.

So why, you ask, are there no true champion fairway wood players? I suspect that the answer lies in the fact that the world's best golfers are able to hit the ball so far these days that they rarely need to take the clubhead cover off a three- or four-wood. Except on rare occasions, the one- and two-irons have replaced the wooden clubs as far as the Weiskopfs and Nicklauses are concerned. Thus, they rarely put in any concentrated practice with these clubs, and at monster holes where they feel compelled to 'have a go' with a three-wood, hit wild shots with surprising regularity simply because they are trying to give the swing that little bit extra in order to eat up just a few more yards. Next time you are at a major tournament where there is a hole requiring even the best players to hit timber from the fairway, just count how many of the professionals hook their second shots! It is all rather comforting for the long handicap golfer.

In the vast majority of professionals' golf bags you will see only

5   A perfect pre-impact position from one of the world's great champions. A veteran perhaps, but still sparing nothing

two woods – the driver and the four-wood, which is useful for hitting long shots from light rough – but there will also be two wedges, and in an increasing number of cases, a one-iron.

So, simply on the grounds that we do not have sufficient opportunity to see today's champions wielding fairway woods, we must turn to one of the great champions of the past to see how it's done – Sam Snead.

Each year, in Britain and America, the Senior Professional Championships are played; the respective winners meeting and playing off for the World Seniors' title. In 1964 the winner of the British event, limited to players of fifty years and over, was Syd Scott – a club professional at Roehampton, near London, but a tournament regular in the 1950s who had competed in the Ryder Cup and was runner-up in the 1954 Open Championship. The American counterpart tournament was won by the amazing Sam Snead, possibly the sweetest-swinger of all time, who was then fifty-two years old.

The match-play decider between these two for the World title was set for Wentworth, where Snead had happy memories. It was here in 1956 that he had partnered the immortal Ben Hogan to victory in the Canada Cup (now renamed the World Cup), and it seemed that the entire population of southern England travelled to the course in order to watch these two legendary characters of golf.

But in 1964, it was a very different Wentworth that awaited Snead. Prolonged heavy rain meant that water oozed to the surface as the players walked to the first tee, and the course's 7,000 yards were a daunting prospect even for the long-hitting Snead. There must have been another worry in his mind, too. Advancing years had taken their toll on his putting nerves. He admitted that he had privately experimented with the 'croquet' method, in which a T-shaped putter is swung between the legs so that the players eyes are directly behind the line of putt. He had been delighted with the results, but was not prepared to putt croquet-style publicly ' 'cos folks'll laugh at me.' And already there was talk of croquet putting being made illegal, which it was a year or so later. At Wentworth, Snead used a conventional centre-shafted putter.

They used to call him Slammin' Sam, and even now – although he is over sixty – Snead's enduring swing is capable of giving the ball a tremendous ride. Despite the length of Wentworth on this particular occasion, he decided that he could forgo a little of his power for the sake of keeping the ball in play, and used a three-wood almost exclusively from the tee. Scott is no mean golfer, and his action gives him a lot of topspin on his drives, so even in these wet conditions he was getting the maximum amount of run from the rain-soaked fairways. Yet it was no contest from the tee, for Snead consistently pitched his three-wood 20 or 30 yards past where Scott's ball had finished.

The long 17th and 18th holes must be familiar to nearly every golfer in Britain. They have appeared on television more times than almost any other holes in the world, for they have provided countless dramas in the Piccadilly World Match-play Championship. With plenty of run on the ball, they are both about reachable for the longest hitters, assuming the power players are prepared to have a go and risk the dangers on either side.

But on this lowering morning, with the threat of yet another downpour, they were surely out of range even for Nicklaus. Snead hit a three-wood from the 17th tee into the perfect position – just right of centre. Another three-wood, and his ball rolled across the right edge of the green and down the bank, pin high. A delicate pitch shot, and in went the putt for an amazing birdie. At the 18th, two incredible three-woods found the heart of the green, and his putt for an eagle stopped half a roll short of the hole. Had it dropped, he would have covered the back nine in 30 strokes.

Poor Syd Scott stuck to his guns as gamely as he could, but he was no match for the precision power of Snead's three-wood, and the end of this 36-hole encounter came on the 12th green in the afternoon.

Ten years have passed since then, in which time Snead has won the World Seniors' title on another three occasions. Galleries in America still have the occasional chance to see him in action in major tournaments. In 1965 he became the oldest winner of an American tournament by winning the Greensboro Open, and on his rare sorties back to the tour, he usually finishes in the top ten in any event.

Even with his unique 'sidesaddle' putting method, in which he faces the hole and uses a centre-shafted putter outside his right foot, Snead would not claim to be the world's best holer-out. So what is

6 and 7   Snead at 60; smooth and economical, but certainly not an 'old man's swing'. When he chooses to venture on to the American circuit, he can still play with today's best

it about his game that prompted Arnold Palmer to remark: 'Who even wants to play that good when you're sixty?'

The answer lies in a marvellously orthodox golf swing, combined with perfect timing. Unlike so many of the modern players, Snead has never demanded power from his golf swing, never put any physical strain on it. As a young man, great length came quite naturally to him, just by swinging the club easily and letting the timing do the work.

This is what makes him an object lesson for every club golfer who doubts what the professionals tell us – that a smooth, well-timed swing

will send the ball further and straighter than a lashing action used in an attempt to hit the ball a country mile. Also, it explains why he is such a good fairway wood player. His innate sense of rhythm success-fully resists the temptation to give the swing that little bit extra.

Snead's Method
Sam Snead's method can best be described as perfectly orthodox: he exhibits all the fundamentals that every teacher of golf tries to instil in his pupils. At the address position, grip, stance and posture are all straight out of the text-book. At the top of the swing, he has made a full turn – with his left shoulder pointed at the ball and the clubhead pointing straight at the target. Through the ball, he keeps the club-head travelling straight along the target-line for as long as possible

before completing the shot in a perfectly relaxed and balanced finish.

But one thing that does help him retain the swing that first took the golf world by storm before the war, is his remarkable physical condition. Snead has continued to exercise gently in order to keep his legs and back muscles supple, and even today, maintains that he possesses the highest leg kick in American golf – it is one of his party tricks! This suppleness enables him to make a full shoulder turn, keeping the arc of the swing wide – an ability that most middle-aged golfers lose only because they imagine that their muscles will not allow them to do it.

Snead closes his stance slightly on all wooden shots by drawing the right foot back an inch or so from the target-line. He maintains that this helps him to turn the hips more easily on the backswing, and helps to keep the clubhead on an inside plane. With a three-wood, the ball is positioned, relative to the feet, in the accepted spot – about an inch inside the left heel.

The real object of nominating Snead as one of the all-time great fairway-wood players, is to consider for a moment the vital element of rhythm. Every golf swing has its own tempo, dependent to some extent on the shape of the swing, but to a much greater degree on the personality of the golfer himself. On any golf course on any Sunday morning one is almost bound to hear one golfer telling another: 'You're swinging too fast.' What he really means is that his companion is swinging faster than he does, and so it looks fast.

The tempo of the swing is as personal as a thumbprint, and every player has to discover for himself his natural rhythm. It is quite possible to swing too *slowly*, and so lose the fluidity and tempo of the entire movement.

Snead is the product of slow-talkin', equable, West Virginian hillbilly stock, and the lazy tempo of his swing truly reflects his personality. But with the fairway woods, particularly, he seems to be swinging well within himself, secure in the knowledge that an accurate contact and smooth timing will send the ball just as far as he wants it to go.

The three- and four-woods may not be vitally significant to the masters of today's game, but they are the standby clubs of the club golfer. As new golf courses are built longer and longer, the handicap player is going to have to use these clubs more and more to cope with the distance problem.

And the four-wood is an immensely versatile weapon. It can cope with fairly thick rough, always assuming that there are no tufts behind the ball blocking the path of the clubhead. It can extract you from wiry heather, which all too easily wraps itself around the head of an iron club. And it can be used as a kind of long pitching club, where power and elevation are required to stay on the putting surface.

The fairway woods tend to be underused by handicap golfers, who generally do not consider doing what Snead did at Wentworth – using a three-wood from the tee at troublesome driving holes. Losing a yard or two in distance is surely a better alternative to losing a ball in the trees!

What every golfer can learn from Snead is that the fairway woods have to be *swung* and not hit. That may be true of nearly all golf shots, but with these clubs in particular, we are always faced with a long shot, usually to a green, and there is the ever-present tendency to try to over-reach ourselves.

8   Weiskopf stands very tall to the ball, making the fullest use of his six feet three inches

CHAPTER FOUR

The 1- and 2-irons: Tom Weiskopf

In July 1973 I discovered that I was not cut out to be a tipster. While my lot as a golf watcher and writer has always been a happy one, in common with the rest of the world's workers, I have from time to time cast envious eyes at other people's careers, and thought what wonderful lives they lead.

I have, for instance, pictured myself in the role of racing correspondent, complete with hound's-tooth check and brown trilby, who, after all, only needs to find a couple of reasonably priced winners a week to receive the respect and gratitude of millions. That July I found out in the hardest possible way that I was simply not cut out for the life.

A month earlier, my old friend Tom Scott, editor of *Golf Illustrated*, had asked me to write a preview of the Open Championship, and offered the classic throwaway line 'just pick us the winner in 2,000 words.'

Nor was it simply a question of reaching for my punter's pin and idly stabbing at the list of 569 entrants. I argued, I felt, with logic on the grounds of current form, experience and how well the favourites could tailor their games to the demands of Troon.

Thus was I able to dismiss Tom Weiskopf's chances in one brief paragraph – 'Opens are going to fall to Weiskopf's power and fine putting, but I feel he will make his breakthrough into the superstar class in his own country. Perhaps in a couple of years we shall be nominating him as a potential winner of our championship – but not this time.'

Johnny Miller, fresh from his triumph in the American Open, was even more cursorily despatched on the grounds that he would find conditions at Troon totally alien to him.

When it was all over, I could only plead mitigating circumstances as I ducked the screwed-up betting slips hurled savagely at my head. The preview had been written nearly a month before the event, in the middle of a blazing drought. The advent of heavy rain and the use of a pop-up sprinkler system (which is ruining the character of so many of our great seaside courses) changed Troon from a fiery snake into docile acceptance of shots pitched right at the flag. Conditions, indeed, which were ideal for Weiskopf and Miller – none of which was of any consolation to those who followed this 'expert's' advice at ante-post prices.

Troon 1973 was Weiskopf's Open. He stamped his authority on

9   Tom Weiskopf, Open Champion 1973, and one of the new breed of superstars

it from the outset, became the first winner since Henry Cotton in 1934 to lead after all four rounds, and gave everybody the distinct impression of manipulating the rest of the field to his own advantage. Only once did he briefly lose his head – when he took six at the 9th in his third round to fall three strokes behind Miller.

If a player is judged on how he scores when he is playing badly, then Weiskopf is a very great golfer indeed. During that third round he played his worst golf of the championship. On the back nine his beautiful swing looked just a trifle ragged, and his metronomic tempo faltered. He seemed forever to be blasting from sand or playing pitch shots from well-nigh impossible positions – yet at hole after hole, his putts for pars never deviated from the centre of the cup.

It must have been heartbreaking for his playing partner, Miller, to produce his best golf of the week, establish a three-stroke lead and then see it whittled away until finally he reached the locker-room with a one-shot deficit. Weiskopf must have felt at that point that the outcome of the week was in his stars.

It had taken Weiskopf a long time to emerge as the complete player his talents had always suggested. The turning-point came in the 1972 Piccadilly World Match-play Championship when he comfortably defeated Lee Trevino in the final. Tom's father had recently died, and this seemed to bring about a radical change in his mental approach to the game. It was a more self-contained, self-assured Weiskopf we saw at Wentworth – his sometimes volatile temperament at last under control. From that moment he became one of America's consistent tournament winners, and during 1973 was hardly ever out of contention.

Troon does not rank among the classic championship venues, and is possibly the least liked of Open sites among the top professionals. Before the championship began, Weiskopf said that he did not understand the course, and after he had won, he was quoted as saying that he still did not understand it, nor did he like it very much. This was not meant churlishly, and even its greatest admirers would have to confess that the course has one or two holes that are poor by championship standards.

But during the week of the championship, Weiskopf tried to understand Troon and left the impression that he had played four rounds with his head. True, his driving was almost immaculate, his iron shots aggressive and his putting almost wizardry, but when the golf course forced him on to the defensive he had the equipment to cope with the situation.

It is not a slogger's course; there are one or two holes where a slightly inaccurate drive can be the kiss of death, and when championships are at stake, golfers of Weiskopf's calibre have to think twice before reaching automatically into the bag for a driver.

Troon is perhaps best known for one such hole, the malignant 11th. In terms of length it only just rates as a par five to the power players; if length alone was the criterion, it would be a comfortable enough four for most of the championship contenders. But such is its difficulty, particularly in a cross-wind, that the vast majority of players are happy to lay up short of the green in two and walk to the 12th tee with a par five on their cards.

The tee-shot has to be played over a right-handed dogleg to an angled fairway. And it has to be hit absolutely right. The merest fade, and the ball finishes in head-high gorse; the faint-hearted who are tempted to play a fraction further left in order to ensure carrying the elbow, run the risk of running out of fairway on the left-hand side – and there, too, is an impenetrable mass of gorse. But even after negotiating these problems, the most diabolical part of the hole remains. Now the player is faced with a long shot – a wood if he is trying to reach the green – with the ever-present threat of the railway line pressing in on the right. So close is the low stone wall that the gentlest of breezes can drift the ball over it and, in a hard summer, the ball can bounce along the right edge of the fairway and simply hop over it. By the green, only a few paces separate the perfect shot from the ball out of bounds.

The 11th at Troon probably gets my vote as the most nerve-racking hole in championship golf, for not only is it a hole where one loose shot can drop strokes to par, but it is quite conceivable for even the best players to run up enormous scores here.

Yet this is the hole where Arnold Palmer put the 1962 Open out of the reach of his nearest challengers. By playing a one-iron from the tee, and another to the green, he managed two threes, a four and a five in his four rounds that set an Open Championship record total of 276.

Weiskopf matched that total in 1973, and while he may not have played the 11th with the same flamboyant success, he at least made certain that nobody made ground on him there. Like Palmer eleven years earlier, Weiskopf determined to play this hole with his one-iron. It was a club he used frequently at Troon's difficult driving holes, particularly at the 18th where bunkers left and right reduce the fairway to a narrow ribbon at driver pitching length, and at the 215-yard 17th, where into a freshening wind many competitors were compelled to hit wooden clubs.

It would be less than fair to the rest of his game to single out Weiskopf's big iron play as the foundation stone of his first major championship success. But on a golf course that demanded keeping the ball safely in play, his power and accuracy with the one- and two-irons was certainly a contributory factor.

The one-iron, not surprisingly, is generally the province of big, powerful men. Nicklaus used it almost exclusively from the tee on his way to victory in the 1966 Open, when Muirfield was running very fast and the rough had been allowed to grow to waist-height. And perhaps the finest one-iron shot I have witnessed was made by another giant, Peter Oosterhuis.

At the time Oosterhuis had not yet turned professional and started the climb up the ladder of international stardom. It was May 1967, and Great Britain and Ireland were meeting America's best amateur golfers in the biennial competition for the Walker Cup. The two days of the match laid forever the myth that Americans cannot play in the wind, for the British supporters got just the kind of unpleasant weather they had been hoping for at Royal St George's, Sandwich. Not only did it blow unrelentingly, but there were periodic downpours to further dampen British spirits as the match moved inevitably in the Americans' favour.

The American team had been grossly underrated. It was a mixture of unknown youth and some surprisingly senior representatives who had been tried and tested in the furnace of international competition. Among the more youthful members were such names as Bob Murphy, Bob Dickson, Marty Fleckman and Ron Cerrudo, all of whom turned professional soon afterwards, Murphy with outstanding success.

The 13th at Royal St George's is a 440-yard par four to a difficult hog-backed green. Oosterhuis and Ronnie Shade had opened the batting for Britain and Ireland by taking on Murphy and Cerrudo in the first foursome. They reached the 13th, with the wind howling straight into their faces, and it was there that Oosterhuis hit an unforgettable second shot with a one-iron. As the Americans might say, it flew 'quail high' through the wind as if fired from a rifle fitted with a telescopic sight. Not for one instant did it waver from its line to the flag, finishing a matter of inches away to give the Anglo-Scots pairing a much-needed three, and ultimately a halved match.

The one-iron is certainly not a weapon for the average club golfer, although one or two of the best club players are beginning to discover its value on tight-driving courses. But generally, its lack of loft and small head which demand precision striking if the ball is to fly properly, make it unpopular – and it does make more sense for most handicap golfers to carry a more versatile wooden club that they can handle with confidence.

Many club players also tend to shy away from the two-iron, and among middle handicap golfers, more often than not, it is only those who are used to playing their golf by the sea who give it a regular airing. This is a pity, because apart from being an extremely valuable club in certain conditions – particularly when there is a breeze – there is no more satisfying stroke in golf than a properly struck two-iron flying low and hard at the target.

To a certain extent, it is the often-repeated fallacy that the long irons are the hardest clubs in the bag to play that has led to this mistrust of the two-iron. Yet one has only to look at Weiskopf's swing action to see that the swing is exactly the same as for all the other clubs in the bag. He does not vary his method because he has a long iron in his hand.

Weiskopf stands very tall to the ball, making the fullest use of his six feet three inches. Like Nicklaus, and nearly all the other good players, he concentrates on keeping the swing-arc as wide as possible. This is a very important factor through the ball where the long irons are concerned, for although the ball is positioned two or three inches inside the left heel, it must be hit with a slightly descending blow to achieve a crisp and accurate contact.

The one-piece takeaway, with hands and arms starting the clubhead back in one firm unit, is very pronounced, and he makes a full shoulder turn to take the club into a position at the top where the shaft is parallel to the ground with the clubhead pointing at the target.

Starting the downswing with a forward slide of the hips, Weiskopf gives a strong impression of aiming the heel of his left hand at the back of the ball during the second part of the downswing. The initial movement of the downswing has put him into a late-hitting position, and he maintains that position by keeping the wrists cocked until his hands are below hip-height. Once the hands are released into the shot, Weiskopf makes a conscious effort to keep his right shoulder travelling under his chin, which helps him to achieve the long right

10 and 11   Weiskopf with a two-iron. Like the man, the swing is tall and elegant, but the position of his left wrist at the top of the swing is not for the weekend golfer

arm extension through the ball with the clubhead travelling close to the ground for two or three feet after impact. From there, he moves into a wonderfully fluid and balanced end-of-swing position.

At Troon there was little noticeable difference in the tempo of Weiskopf's swing, whether he was hitting a one-iron low through the wind or a gentle pitch with a wedge. The easy rhythm with which he executes every shot is extremely important with the long irons. While these are power clubs, the size of the head and the degree of loft allow for no mishitting. Weiskopf is content to let the length of the shaft and the width of his arc smoothly build up to maximum acceleration through the ball, without apparently supplying too much physical effort.

42

He seems to give the entire swing plenty of time to fall into place, the even rhythm of the backswing being followed by a slight pause at the top which gives the hips and hands that vital moment to position themselves for the release into the back of the ball. And neither is there any effort on the part of the shoulders to supply that 'little bit extra' in the impact area – a failing that ruins so many handicap golfers' shots when they have big clubs in their hands.

While it is true that the one-iron is exclusively the province of the power specialists, the handicap golfer can add a powerful weapon to his armoury if he overcomes his fear of the two-iron and has confidence in producing a smooth and compact swing. He can do no better than study Weiskopf in action, for here is a classic swing, admirably orthodox, relying on the height of the player and the width of his action to produce power. But the tempo of the swing is of major importance, and it is in this aspect that Weiskopf can teach us most.

12   Graham Marsh. As with all fine players, the backswing is firm and wide, but never out of control

CHAPTER FIVE

The 3- and 4-irons : Graham Marsh

Graham Marsh has yet to prove himself in the super-star class of the world's greatest golfers, but most of those who have followed his career have been left in little doubt that he will ultimately achieve this status. Certainly, he is already an international champion, for like so many Australians before him, Marsh has always been prepared to travel to the four corners of the earth in search of tough tournament competition.

Indeed, Marsh must now be one of the most experienced professionals in the world in terms of golfing conditions outside his own country. He is the only non-Asian to consistently win titles on the gruelling Far East circuit – perhaps the most pressure-packed tour outside the United States – and he has also won in New Zealand, India, Europe and Britain.

He qualified as a schoolteacher in Australia, and developed into one of the country's best amateur golfers. But he made the break from the classroom in 1968 by turning professional at the age of twenty-four. Marsh first made an impact in Europe in 1972, when he competed in just five tournaments – and won two of them in successive weeks. He had won the Swiss Open Championship at Crans-sur-Sierre in 1970 with a score of 274. Two years later he won with a total of 270 in a desperate finish from Tony Jacklin.

Jacklin was the major attraction for the fans that week, and in the end, he gave value for money. But after the first round, the odds against him contesting the finish of the championship must have been very long indeed. He opened with a 74, nine strokes behind the joint leaders, and seven behind Marsh.

The Australian maintained his consistency over the second round with another 67, and while Jacklin's 65 was the best round of the day, it did little to close the gap on the leaders. However, Jacklin's performances once the enthusiasm and inspiration are there bear no resemblance to the indifferent form he had shown in the first round. On the third day he scorched round Crans in a brilliant 64, but while Marsh must have felt the pressure of the rampant Englishman pounding up on him, it was not reflected in his score; his 66 still left him three strokes ahead of Jacklin.

Bravely though he had tried, Jacklin was never quite able to salvage his terrible start to the Championship. His 68 on the last day was just one too many to force a tie with Marsh.

The following week, the circuit moved on to Frankfurt for the

German Open, and this time it was Marsh's turn to shatter the opposition with a brilliant round. He went into the final day tying with Brian Huggett for the lead, and while the little Welshman played with complete composure for a rock-steady 68, Marsh 'went mad' and burned up the Frankfurt course in 64 shots. His victory total of 271 was just one stroke higher than at Crans.

When he came to Britain in 1973, Graham (whose brother Rodney was the current Australian Test wicket-keeper) was already recognized as one of the brightest rising stars in the international game. He enhanced that status at the Sunbeam Electric Scottish Open, played at St Andrews.

This tournament came just a fortnight before the Open at Troon, so many of the overseas stars used it as a serious warm-up event, and it was obvious that whoever won would have to beat some of the best players in the business.

Marsh not only won the tournament, but cake-walked it, and on the last day was so far in front that nobody could offer any kind of serious challenge to him. As he walked from the 16th green in his third round, he was evidently going to lead the field by four or five strokes, but what happened over the next few minutes put the title beyond the grasp of everybody else, and provided spectators and television viewers with one of the most startling finishes ever seen.

The 17th at St Andrews, the Road Hole, is one of the most pernicious and widely discussed holes in golf. Until a few years ago, the drive had to fly over the black railway sheds beyond the out-of-bounds wall on the right, and once the player had successfully negotiated the acute dogleg angle, his problems really began with the fearsome second shot. The black sheds have gone now, to be replaced by a luxury hotel, but if the face of the hole has changed, the questions it asks have not.

Assuming the player has made the safe haven of the fairway, he is then faced with a long iron into a target area that looks the size of a pocket handkerchief. Biting deep into the left front corner of the green is the cavernous Road Bunker, and if he is in that, only a few yards of manicured St Andrews green separates the player from the road that runs a few feet from the right side and the back of the green.

There is no room at all for error. Any second shot held away from the road will almost certainly be gathered by the bunker on the left, and even the merest touch of fade is enough to find oneself trying to play a shot from the hard and gritty road surface with absolutely no chance of stopping the ball on the slick putting surface. The stories of great players hitting shots from one side of the green to the other with the regularity of a pantomime act are legion, and this one hole has dashed more championship aspirations than any other in golf. It is 466 yards of lurking terror, and so fearsome is its reputation that even

13 and 14   The end of an incredible round. Marsh drives from the 18th at St Andrews in the third round of the Scottish Open, and a moment or two later knocks the putt in for an eagle two

47

the world's best usually elect to play the second shot short of the right edge of the green and hope to make their par by chipping and putting.

Even the ice-cool Marsh must have thought of the disasters that this hole has wreaked in the past as he stood on the 17th tee on that grey evening, but his drive flew like an arrow across the out-of-bounds wall and back into the centre of the fairway, and it was then that he showed the go-for-everything assurance that all great champions must possess. Instead of protecting his big lead by laying up short, he aimed straight for the heart of the green with a four-iron, the ball finishing a dozen or so feet away from the hole. When the putt rolled straight in the middle, he had achieved one of the rarest birdies in championship golf.

But the drama was not over yet. Reminiscent of Nicklaus's thundering drive in the Open three years earlier, Marsh crashed into the ball from the 18th tee, and watched with satisfaction as it rolled up on to the green 358 yards away, coming to rest 20 feet right of the flagstick. Those watching round the green in this historic setting were quite sure that he had hit the putt much too hard, but Marsh in this inspired mood does not play safe. The ball slammed into the back of the hole and disappeared like a startled rabbit for an eagle two.

Still with a round to go, the Scottish Open was a foregone conclusion, for Marsh now had an unassailable seven-stroke lead.

He was to feature in one other drama in Britain in 1973. As a result of his performances in Europe, and in recognition of his feat of winning the Order of Merit as the most consistent player on the Far East circuit in 1972, Marsh was invited to join the elite eight who make up the field for the Piccadilly World Match-play Championship at Wentworth. Here was his opportunity to prove that he could hold his own with the super-stars on equal terms, for here were Jacklin, Trevino, Weiskopf and Miller ranged against him. It was an opportunity he grasped with both hands.

He played well throughout the tournament, the length of Wentworth in October placing a premium on his longer iron play; and he putted superbly. If other people were surprised to see him carve his way into the final, he certainly showed no evidence of either surprise or nerves.

Between him and the £10,000 first prize lay only one more obstacle, but a pretty formidable hurdle it seemed to be. Since the inception of the tournament in 1964, Gary Player had appeared in four finals – and won them all. His victims had been Neil Coles, Bob Charles and Jack Nicklaus twice. Now here he was again, looking for his fifth win in ten years.

It was a fine match, with Player fighting back from the brink of defeat over the final few holes, and ultimately needing an eight-footer at the 36th hole to stay alive. He seemed to half-hit the ball, and immediately walked forward in disgust and with an obvious air of resignation. But at the last gasp, it dropped into the hole, and in the gathering gloom, they went to the 37th tee.

So began one of those extraordinary feats of escapology in which

Player seems to revel. Twice in the next three holes, the little South African scraped halves by getting down in two from greenside bunkers, and nobody was made more aware of Player's reputation as the world's best bunker player than poor Graham Marsh.

By the time they reached the 40th hole, a par five, it was almost too dark to see. If the match was not resolved here, play would obviously have to be suspended until the following day. Marsh hit a fine second thirty feet behind the hole, and once again Player was bunkered on the left of the green. He splashed out to eight feet, and in almost total darkness, the Australian putted to a yard. Player, fighting for his life, holed; Marsh missed.

If proof were needed of Marsh's tremendous potential, it was supplied that week at Wentworth. Without winning one of the great championships of the world, he had firmly established himself among the top dozen players.

It is difficult to point to his strengths, for he has few weaknesses. But as his four-iron to the St Andrews Road Hole was one of the shots of the year, and he played his three- and four-irons with consummate ease and authority at Wentworth, his method with these clubs should be studied.

His set-up position is perfectly orthodox, with the ball positioned two or three inches inside his left heel. He uses a lot of leg action throughout the swing, and ensures plenty of freedom in the lower part of his body by keeping the knees well flexed and unlocked at the address position.

As with all fine players, the backswing is firm and wide, but never out of control. He takes the club back in the classic one-piece action, with arms, hands and clubhead all moving together in a solid unit. Like all today's power players, he relies on a big body turn to help generate maximum clubhead speed at impact, and at the top of the backswing his left shoulder is tucked under his chin and his back pointing at the target. To assist in this big turn, he allows his hips to turn more than many players, but his fast leg action gets them back into the correct position at impact.

At the top, Marsh is very solid, with the left hand firmly in control and his left wrist straight. Despite the extent of his turn, the club never quite reaches the horizontal.

The legs and hips dominate the downswing; the rapid weight transference from right to left and consequent hip slide bring him into a good attacking position behind the ball from where he can swing through freely with the right hand and arm. The long right arm extension after impact is very noticeable.

Altogether, Marsh's action suggests a freedom of swing, combined with firmness of hand action. The hands are always firmly in control and dominating the striking of the ball, but his big body movement is helping to put his hands in a position from where they can do their job most efficiently.

Since Peter Thomson first achieved international stardom in the 1950s, there has been a constant, though relatively small, stream of super golfing talent coming from Australia. Bruce Crampton has dedicated himself to the rigours of the American circuit, and after years of trying, is now reaping the rich rewards of his arduous life there. Bruce Devlin, too, has done extremely well over the years in America, but is less committed to the United States. His beautifully rhythmic swing

15 and 16   Marsh with a four-iron. He has a big shoulder and hip turn on the backswing, and a lot of forward hip movement on the through-swing. A beautiful right arm extension through the ball

has helped him to achieve fame and fortune, but thus far, none of the world's major titles. Another Australian who could go right to the top is David Graham, who also plays much of his golf nowadays in America.

But I believe Graham Marsh could prove to be the best of them all. He has both the temperament and the game to take on the world's best, and he is now at the optimum age for the breakthrough into super-stardom.

CHAPTER SIX

The 5- and 6-irons: Johnny Miller

In June 1973 there was a day of the most pulverizing significance to the golf world. For on that day a twenty-six-year-old flaxen-haired golfer with film-star looks won the American Open Championship. In itself that might not have been remarkable, but Johnny Miller's final round of 63 over the tough Oakmont course in Pennsylvania reverberated throughout the game, wherever golf is played, and heralded one of the most exciting careers in the new league of the super-stars. This was almost certainly the finest round ever played in a championship.

Pennsylvania is the home state of the living legend, Arnold Palmer. So, perhaps not surprisingly, the championship reached fever-pitch after three rounds, for here was the great man tied for the lead and in a position to win his first major title since his Masters victory in 1964. The US Open has not been Palmer's luckiest tournament, for after his victory at Denver in 1960, he had failed three times in play-offs – to Nicklaus, Julius Boros and Casper.

At Oakmont, Arnie's Army, swelled to enormous proportions, had no doubts that their hero would soon be crowned Open Champion once again. They gave little thought to the other joint leaders – the amazing Julius Boros who had defeated Palmer and Jackie Cupit in a play-off for the 1963 Open, his second victory, and who now, at the age of fifty-three, was swinging the club as lazily and economically as he had thirty years ago; and Jerry Heard and John Schlee, who had been paired together in the third round and had scored 66 and 67 respectively.

Certainly, Arnie's Army were in no way concerned with Johnny Miller. His first two rounds had kept him nicely in the hunt – efforts of 71 and 69 – but in round three he had produced one of his familiar lapses, a 76 which had dropped him six strokes behind the joint leaders and left a total of twelve players ahead of him. This had become a familiar pattern for Miller, who since turning professional in 1969, might have won several tournaments if he had been able to exclude just one bad round from his four. To some extent this Achilles heel was rectified by inspirational rounds, and on these occasions there seemed to be no limit to Miller's low scoring. More often than not, however, the one bad round had left him too much to do.

His situation at Oakmont was surely irretrievable, for on a championship course against the world's best opposition at the peak of their form, no man can look for a second bite at the cherry when he has dropped himself so far out of contention.

Yet as Miller stood on the tee at the short 13th on the final day, only the most faithful of Arnie's Army were still following Palmer, and as news filtered back to the leaders of what was going on well ahead of them, more and more spectators ran forward to catch up with Johnny Miller.

He had completed the first twelve holes with five pars and an incredible seven birdies, cutting a swath through the giant leader boards sited all over the course. It was a prodigious performance, with Miller's long, freewheeling swing crashing his drives down the fairways, his iron shots beaded unwaveringly at the flags no matter how difficult their positioning, and putts repeatedly dropping into the centre of the holes on Oakmont's fast greens.

From here on, par golf would give him a 65, but would it be good enough to win the Open? The par-three 13th was the clincher, the moment when Miller really knew for the first time that he was in a winning position. His five-iron from the tee never deviated from the line, finishing five feet away, and his eighth birdie of the round was almost a formality. Another medium iron to the par-four 14th left him only nine feet from the cup, but this time the putt did not drop.

The 15th at Oakmont is a tough par four measuring 453 yards. Miller annihilated it. Without holding anything back, he smashed his drive almost 300 yards down the fairway, and as he had done all the way round, aimed straight at the flag with his six-iron. A six-foot putt, and birdie number nine was safely in the bag. Now, at last, he led the Open field – but with his chief rivals still well behind him on the course.

After a standard par at the 16th, he came to the 17th, an innocuous par four of only 322 yards, the main problem being the double-tiered green. Of all the holes at Oakmont, this one offered the greatest birdie potential. Miller's little pitch shot finished eight feet away, but once again the putt slipped by. And at the difficult 18th, he again played a heroic shot with his six-iron to within fifteen feet, and this time the putt lipped out of the hole.

Had Miller done enough to win the Open with this marvellous round of 63 that could so easily have been the first sub-60 round in a championship? Ultimately, he had, for while Schlee played extraordinarily well for his 70 (and 280 total), the vital putts refused to drop. Those who saw it rated him one of the unluckiest runners-up in a major championship. But as every golfer knows, only the figures count, and the 1973 US Open went to Miller at 279, with Schlee at 280 and Tom Weiskopf 281.

In the time taken to set words into type and get the presses rolling, the golf world knew that it had a new champion capable of inspirational brilliance rarely seen before. Quoting the immortal words of Weiskopf: 'Johnny Miller? I didn't even know Miller had made the cut.'

Had it been any other young professional this result might have been considered a flash in the pan without the accolades of super-stardom being laid upon his shoulders. With Miller it was different. In his three full years as a professional, he had shown himself capable of almost superhuman rounds fashioned with the kind of exciting genius that had been lacking from the pro circuit since the heyday of Palmer.

In January 1970, when he had been a professional only three months, Miller produced a third round of 61 in the Phoenix Open. His playing partner, Jim Jamieson, described him as 'unlucky'. 'It could have been a 57 or 58 if some lipped-out putts had dropped,' Jamieson told the waiting pressmen. The following year Miller discovered that 'I could play with the big boys' when two closing rounds of 68 gave him a tie for second place behind Charles Coody in the Masters, and later in 1971 he won the Southern Open by the huge margin of five strokes after rounds of 65, 67, 68, 67.

In 1972 the pattern of brilliance and mediocrity within the four rounds of the same tournament became almost a standard feature of his scoring. He began the year by losing a play-off to Nicklaus for the Bing Crosby tournament after rounds of 75, 68, 67 and 74, finished the US Open in seventh place after a disastrous last round of 79 over Pebble Beach and then scored 76, 66, 72, 75 during the Open Championship at Muirfield, his professional debut in Britain.

But after his victory at Oakmont, and the new prestige that only an Open Champion acquires, his bad round that had plagued so many tournament results, miraculously disappeared. There emerged a player of the very highest stature with a repertoire able to make even Nicklaus pale by comparison. A fortnight after Oakmont he played supremely well to fight Weiskopf all the way to the line in the Troon Open, and he completed 1973 by winning the individual aggregate in the World Cup. Then came a month's break from competitive golf, only re-starting with the 1974 US circuit.

Miller made history in the first three weeks of 1974 by winning all three tournaments – the Bing Crosby, the Phoenix Open and the Tucson Open – during which he broke par in every round, and started at Tucson with a ten under par 62. Three weeks' work had earned him $100,000.

It is not hard to predict that Johnny Miller, who like Casper is a devout Mormon, will become the richest golfer of all time. American prize money has reached a zenith, yet all the money he wins on the world's golf courses will represent only petty cash by comparison with his advertising endorsements. For not only has he been blessed with a remarkably exhilarating golf game, but he was 'born pretty', as the Americans say. Not only is he the darling of every female member of the gallery – although he is a happily married family man – but he is very much the darling of American advertising agencies.

In a golfer so talented, it is hard to select one particular department of the game to nominate as his strength. Miller drives beautifully – very long and very straight – hits his irons with perfect precision, and putts as though he had never missed one in his life. But perhaps his breakthrough at Oakmont, and his subsequent play at Troon, was

17 Johnny Miller's good looks will probably earn him more in advertising endorsements than he could ever earn on the golf course

dependent on his mid-iron play more than anything else. After all, it was a five-iron that produced the birdie that proved crucial at Oakmont's 13th, and a six-iron that wrapped up the title two holes later.

Miller's game combines power with subtlety, but for him the five- and six-irons are accuracy clubs rather than distance clubs. Every time he has a mid-iron in his hands, he feels that he is setting up a potential birdie chance. His position at Oakmont after three rounds compelled him to attack the flags aggressively with these clubs, and Weiskopf's robot-like play at Troon also demanded precision

approaches to the greens. Both courses provided him with receptive putting surfaces which allowed him to aim straight at the holes, ignoring the bunkering and other problems that surrounded the greens.

Today's super-stars are increasingly represented by the sweet swingers of golf. The idiosyncratic swings of Palmer, Gay Brewer, Doug Sanders and Miller Barber enable them to play fine golf from time to time, and still to win the occasional tournaments. With each year that passes, however, it becomes more noticeable that the most consistent results, the most regular tournament victories in the un-ending grind of tournament golf, come from swings that are secure in their orthodoxy and consistent in their tempo. Miller is genuinely representative of this category, and his swing, so full now of youthful athleticism, is so sound that he should be able to temper it with advancing years.

Miller's action can best be described as 'freewheeling' – it is long, loose and fluid. With his long shots he makes a very full turn on the backswing; so big is his turn, in fact, that there is a slight tendency to overswing, although he always retains control of the clubhead by keeping a firm left-hand grip at the top. A fast hip and leg action on the downswing helps him into a good position to hit the ball; and in

18 (page 57), 19 and 20   The freedom and length of Miller's swing with a driver is reminiscent of Snead in his heyday

the impact area, he pours every available ounce of power straight through the ball and on towards the target.

That is the swing that impresses spectators so much when he wants to lash the ball 300 yards off the tee. With his medium irons, he is much more concerned with accuracy, yet the fluid, freewheeling effect of his action is not restrained to the point where he is guiding the ball through the air. Miller produces his most awesome strokes when he is under pressure and forced to go for everything, this is when his adrenalin flows. And it is this aggression that translates into his wonderfully free action.

With the medium irons, he sets himself up with the ball just ahead of the centre point between his feet, and with a narrower stance than

21 and 22   Even with the 'control' clubs, like the five- and six-iron, Miller is not afraid to swing freely at the ball, and give it everything he's got

he would use with a driver. This effectively restricts his body action slightly, which in turn reduces the length of the backswing to a point just short of the parallel. Even so, he makes a big shoulder turn, so that at the top of the swing his left shoulder is tucked under his chin. The downswing is started with the typical hip-slide so characteristic of most of the world's best players, and he keeps the right elbow tucked in close to the side for as long as possible.

Miller delays the hand action with these iron shots by pulling the club *down* towards the ball with the left hand, the heel of the palm aimed at the back of the ball. This very late-hitting position guaran-

tees the important sequence of contact, ball first, then the turf, which not only gives an accurate strike, but helps to impart the backspin club golfers admire so much in the professionals.

Through the ball, Miller keeps his head riveted and hits right through with his right arm towards the target with the right shoulder passing smoothly under his chin. Even on these controlled shots, he allows his swing to move through into the full-follow-through position so beloved by cameramen.

Of course, every top-class professional has to be good with his medium irons if he is going to shave strokes off par. But I doubt whether any player in 1973 hit such a high proportion of these long approach shots so close to the hole with such devastating results. There are two things that the handicap golfer can learn from this example: first, that the game is never over until the final putt is in the hole, and second, that when all is apparently lost, a free and aggressive attitude can sometimes turn the tide. Johnny Miller proved both points at Oakmont. Among even the very best professionals, most would have played the last round merely in order to maintain their position had they been in Miller's position. He, on the other hand, was not satisfied to settle for 13th place and its rewards. He set out to tear the course apart in a do-or-die effort, and if he was fortunate to find the putts dropping on that particular day, who could begrudge him his fortune when he had been prepared to stake everything on a hopeless gamble? Whether his reservoir of inspiration will dry up over the years, only time will tell. Currently, he remains golf's most exciting phenomenon, the natural successor to Nicklaus. And with such tremendous talents as Ben Crenshaw, Lanny Wadkins and Jerry Heard among the younger brigade of America's professionals, one can predict that these four may become the Big Four during the 1970s and into the 1980s.

CHAPTER SEVEN

The 7- and 8-irons : Tony Jacklin

The greatest individual influences on British golf since the war have
been Arnold Palmer and Tony Jacklin. It was Palmer's victory in
the 1961 Open Championship at Royal Birkdale that first exposed
the British public to this American folk-hero who was already a living
legend to spectators and television viewers in his home country.

In 1959 there was not one prominent American professional among
the 285 entries for the Muirfield Open. In 1960 Palmer came to
St Andrews to play in the event for the first time, and failed by a
stroke to catch the popular Australian, Kel Nagle. But his win at
Birkdale gave the championship a prestige that had been lacking
since before the war. If Palmer made this annual pilgrimage to the
wild seaside courses of Britain, then the British Open was an event
in which the elite of America's professionals had to play. During the
early 1960s, Palmer did more for the British Open Championship
than could have been achieved by anyone else.

There was another important side-effect of his presence. The
British people were soon caught up in the Palmer legend, and the
Anglo-Scots legions of Arnie's Army were no less idolatrous than their
American counterparts. Nothing makes better television than a great
personality and mass support for him. And so major golf was televised
for the first time, and suddenly millions of uninitiated people were
exposed to the game for the first time. Perhaps it is not stretching the
point too far to say that Palmer was largely responsible for the
enormous participant golf boom of the 1960s.

Throughout the decade, the Open Championship continued to
grow in stature, television continued to cover major events, more
and more column inches were devoted to coverage of the game in the
daily papers, the flood-tide of new golfers increased at an un-
precedented rate and British manufacturers of golf equipment made
record sales. But there was something missing : British pride.

There was no home player who could seriously threaten the world
supremacy of the Palmers, the Players, the Nicklauses or the Caspers
– not, that is, until Tony Jacklin came along.

I believe I can claim to be the first writer to interview Jacklin, who
at the time was a totally unknown name. He was nineteen years old
and had just won a minor professional event in Middlesex when I
met him in the clubhouse at Potters Bar, where he was assistant to
Bill Shankland. In the course of our conversation he said that he was
going to be the best golfer in the world, and then calmly outlined

how he planned to achieve that status. It was about then that Cassius Clay was telling an ever-receptive press 'I am the greatest!' and as every hopeful young assistant golfer harbours dreams of fame and fortune, it would have been easy to dismiss Jacklin's cool announcement as so much pie in the sky. But even then, there was something in his manner and in his conviction that suggested he was made of sterner stuff.

Six years later, Jacklin had won the Open Championship, had halved the vital final single against Nicklaus to give Britain and Ireland a tie in the Ryder Cup at Royal Birkdale, and still holding his Open Championship title was to win the US Open at the Hazel-

23 *The perfect example of staying behind the ball – Jacklin from the rough*

tine Club, Minneapolis, by the enormous margin of seven strokes. What Palmer had started in 1960, Jacklin continued into the 1970s. As with Palmer, there is a sense of the dramatic about Jacklin's play. Who but Jacklin, for instance, could launch his international career by winning the Dunlop Masters, at the same time becoming the first player to hole in one live on British television? Who but Jacklin could hole a vast putt right across the 17th green against Nicklaus to ensure a tied match against the Americans in the Ryder Cup? Who but Jacklin could win the US Open by seven strokes, holing from the length of the green at the last hole? Who but Jacklin could tear the front nine at St Andrews apart by opening the defence of his Open Championship with a first nine score of 29? Who but Jacklin could win two motor cars with one shot during an American tournament in which he finished 62nd? And who but Jacklin could restore faith in his flagging 'young lion' image by returning to the scene of his first great victory and winning the Jacksonville Open for the second time in four years?

His play is all the more dramatic because he is capable of playing listlessly one week, and then spurring himself to brilliance for the big occasion the next. Now that he has drastically reduced his appearances in the United States, the 'big ones' for Jacklin are the Open and the Ryder Cup. It is on these great international occasions that he delves within himself for inspiration that is rarely seen in run-of-the-mill tournaments.

I do not believe that he has fulfilled the promise he made himself as a nineteen-year-old. Even when he held the Open Championships of both Britain and America at the same time, I doubt whether he was *the* best player in the world. The mark of greatness is to win the 'big ones' and then to maintain that kind of form against the echelons of smaller fry who would usurp your crown. It is much easier to make the breakthrough to a level of superiority than to stay at that level for a long period of time.

Most who have followed his career would probably agree that the ability is still there, that he could still be the greatest. But since his victory at Hazeltine his objectives may have changed. Now he has all the trappings of a wealthy young man – a mansion in Gloucestershire, a Rolls-Royce, invitations to shoot over the country's best estates – but he does not seem to have the burning desire of a Palmer to go on proving himself, to win for the sheer delight of winning. It is purely a matter of temperament, and who can blame him for choosing his own life?

Even so, Jacklin numbers among the world's great champions, and never more so than when he tees up in the Open Championship. He has a game particularly suited to our big seaside courses, and one should remember that his victory at Hazeltine was achieved in a high wind that blew the rest of the field to oblivion while he produced rounds of 71, 70, 70, 70.

At Lytham in 1969 Tony Jacklin joined the world's elite. As he pushed his way through the wildly cheering crowds scrambling up the 18th fairway, he looked like Caesar returning to Rome, dressed from head to foot in purple. It had been a courageous performance, for in his third round he had not played his best. At hole after hole on the back nine he had splashed out of greenside bunkers and holed the putts for life-saving pars, and on the following day none of his immediate rivals were able to make the birdie putts that could rob him of his first Open Championship.

In 1970 the Open was at St Andrews. Jacklin arrived to defend his title straight from America with the US Open trophy tucked away in his suitcase. He looked hollow-eyed and strained; the toll on his sleep had been heavy.

As we watched from behind the first green, the defending champion rolled in a putt of ten feet for a birdie. That, we said to ourselves, is a great way to start a title defence. But when a five-footer went in at the second, and another from ten feet at the third for a 3, 3, 3 start, we knew that we were in for a Jacklin 'special'. By the time he holed his wedge shot to the 9th for an eagle, to be out in 29, our senses were so numbed by what we had seen that it came as no great surprise.

After ten holes he was eight under par, and so rapt were we by this display, that nobody noticed the ghost of Young Tom Morris stirring over the sea. Surely, it could only have been Young Tom who saved the hallowed Old Course from such impertinent savagery? As the storm broke, so the magic spell was broken. At 7.30 the following morning we trudged out in the sheeting rain to the 14th to watch Jacklin finish his round in 6, 4, 5, 5, 4 for a 67.

Who knows what might have happened if he had been able to complete that first round while the adrenalin was still pouring through his veins? Would he have tired as he so obviously did towards the end of the championship? Who knows . . . But the record books show that he finished with a 76 to be three strokes behind Nicklaus and Sanders.

He came even closer to regaining his title in 1971, when only Trevino's merciless putting over the bumpy Royal Birkdale greens staved off Lu Hiang Huan by one shot, and Jacklin by two. And then in 1972 he played possibly his finest golf ever in the Open, only to be robbed on Muirfield's 71st green by Trevino's chip-in.

It is this ability to turn on his inspiration in the world's oldest – and still, in my opinion, greatest – championship, that makes Tony Jacklin one of golf's super-stars. That, and the ability to flight the ball through the wind on championship linksland courses.

When he is playing well, Jacklin has no obvious weaknesses in his game – although, like Palmer, he is obsessed with his 'inability' to putt, which is more mental pressure than real. In assessing his greatest strength, I pick the seven- and eight-irons because these clubs have been at the heart of so many of his great performances. All top-class professionals play these clubs well, for they give golden opportunities of birdies. But when Jacklin is in inspirational form, he consistently hits these long pitch shots extraordinarily close.

This shot played an important part in yet another dramatic Jacklin performance – over Wentworth's 'Burma Road' in the semi-finals of the 1972 Piccadilly World Match-play Championship. This was a needle contest, for his opponent was Lee Trevino, who only three months earlier had wrenched the Open Championship trophy from Jacklin's grasp in that devastating instant at Muirfield.

The matches at Wentworth are played over 36 holes, and at the halfway stage the contest was over bar the shouting. Trevino had completed the West Course in 67, seven under par, and held a four-up lead at lunch. But in the afternoon, pure magic flowed through Jacklin's iron clubs – particularly the seven- and eight-irons – and at hole after hole the ball settled only a foot or two from the flagstick. Once again, Jacklin reached the turn in 29, just as he had at St Andrews two years previously, and he had turned a four-hole deficit into a one-hole lead.

Still the birdies came from both sides as Jacklin and Trevino battled their way towards the clubhouse over Wentworth's punishingly long second nine, but the crucial hole was the very last. Trevino hit two woods into the green and two-putted for his birdie; Jacklin pitched from left of the green, and a beautifully struck putt just refused to drop. Jacklin had completed the course in 63, and Trevino in his second 67 of the day.

Jacklin's technique with the 'long short irons' is to punch the ball relatively low at the target, an ideal method on seaside courses. The flight is much less affected by the breeze than is the high, towering shot; maximum backspin is applied even on the firm, fast putting surfaces.

Jacklin rarely hits these clubs flat-out, being much more concerned with accuracy, control and elevation than he is with power. He can hit a full eight-iron about 150 yards, but when he is punching it low at the flag, he would not normally use this club from more than 130 yards.

The technique, one that most amateur golfers find difficult to co-ordinate, depends on dragging the clubhead into the ball with the left hand in such a way that the clubface is hooded at impact, and the ball is struck before the turf divot is taken. To get the ball quickly into the air on a more typical pitch shot, the professionals cock the wrists fairly quickly on the backswing. But with this particular stroke, Jacklin keeps the left wrist firm, without allowing it to become rigid as he takes the club back from the ball, positioned centrally in his relatively narrow stance.

In fact, the one-piece takeaway is much the same as for the longer shots, apart from the fact that the ball positioning has kept the hands slightly ahead of the blade of the club at the initial address position. Rather than the wrist and hand stroke of the high-flying pitch, this is a definite *arm* stroke, with the wrists playing little active part.

The backswing is short and compact, the hands only travelling as high as the shoulders, with the flexed knees giving the body as much freedom as it needs to make this three-quarter swing. The left hand and arm dominate the whole swing, with the left hand pulling the

24 and 25   When Tony Jacklin uses a pitching club, there is little conscious body movement, just a slight 'give' in the knees

clubhead towards the ball, and through the impact area. At the same time, Jacklin has allowed his knees to slide forward and through the shot while keeping his head behind the ball.

The effect of this knee slide and left-hand domination is that at impact the hands are well ahead of the ball, hooding the clubface, and at the same time the clubhead is travelling *down and through* the shot, giving the important ball/turf striking sequence. The left hand must continue to pull the clubhead through after impact, with the

back of the left wrist pointing at the target. From this position it is virtually impossible to continue the swing into the classical high follow-through position, unless the player allows the right hand to dominate the through-swing after impact, which could lead to a dangerous scooping action. For this reason, Jacklin keeps the follow-through short and blocked, with the clubhead following the path of the ball for as long as the left wrist can stay firm.

This punch shot is one that the club golfer finds very hard to master, chiefly because of the co-ordination required between the knees and the left arm to ensure that the hands are leading the clubhead into the ball with the face square to the target. One can easily drag the heel of the club into the ball, rather than the striking area of the face, resulting in golf's most harassing shot – the shank. The other difficulty often experienced is in the timing of the shot. The delivery has to be crisp and firm, yet made from a much more compact swing than is usual. This leads many golfers to try to add a little more muscle to the stroke, and almost automatically destroy control. For this reason Jacklin uses a bigger club than he would normally need to achieve the same distance, thus he swings at a very even tempo. Indeed, he gives the impression of swinging down and through the ball at the same speed as his backswing, the firmness of the stroke being completely controlled by the left hand.

To perfect this stroke (which can equally well be adapted to the nine-iron or even the pitching wedge in the hands of a good player) needs a great deal of practice and plenty of confidence. But once learnt, it is golf's most effective stroke in the wind. Fortunately, for most club golfers, there is an alternative. Less lofted clubs can be used for traditional pitch-and-run shots, the only disadvantage being that the player has to judge the amount of roll on the ball after touchdown. The punched approach shot carries maximum backspin, and can be made to stop as quickly as a well-struck pitching wedge.

CHAPTER EIGHT

The 9-iron: Lu Liang Huan

The nine-iron is the handicap golfer's friend. Apart from his putter, he probably uses this club more than any in the bag. For the majority of his pitches within a radius of 110 yards from the flag, the nine-iron is an almost automatic choice; when he is chipping from just off the edge of the green, this is a popular club; and even when in the trees at the edge of the fairway, as often as not it is the trusty nine-iron that is called upon to extricate the ball.

One October evening a few years ago, the nine-iron became my most trusted friend, too. If I may digress for a moment, I will recount the story of how that club and I fought a duel with Dracula in the dank autumnal dusk . . . and we won!

A British airline had organized a tournament for up-and-coming young professionals at the charming Leatherhead Golf Club in Surrey. The main event was preceded by a pro–am in which I found myself paired with the nine Scottish professional, Walter Slaven. We teed off at about nine in the morning, and a little over three hours later, yours truly was sinking his first pint in the bar. The course had been kind to me, and my nine-iron and wedge had worked well at several of the shortish par fours. My round of 71 obviously stood a chance in the scratch amateur section.

If the course had been kind, the sponsors were kinder. After a couple more beers and gins, we had a fine lobster lunch, liberally washed down with excellent white wine. After lunch, with competitors still going off from the first tee, Arthur Crawley-Boevey, the Professional Golfers' Association tournament administrator asked me if I would stay around for the prizegiving that evening, because my score still led in that section.

Well, what is one to do with an afternoon when both the company and the bar are so convivial? Arthur stopped by our table at about six o'clock in the evening.

'Christopher Lee has just come in and tied your score. Looks as though you'll have to get yourself ready for a play-off,' he said.

At first I thought he was joking. I could only mumble something unintelligible, which in view of our friendship, was probably just as well. Hardly able to stand, let alone swing a golf club, the last thing I could contemplate was a sudden-death play-off in the fast-gathering gloom of the Surrey countryside with a man who has made Count Dracula the most terrifying of the screen's horror villains.

My companions poured coffee down me at a rate that would have thrilled the Brazilian plantation owners.

The play-off was to take the form of the most sudden of sudden-deaths. Arthur Crawley-Boevey was to pace out 120 yards from the flagstick at the 18th when we would each have one shot, and the nearest to the hole was the winner. Soon it would be completely dark. When Arthur finished pacing and indicated the spot, I found myself looking into a wall of blackness. Only the clubhouse lights were visible; there was no sign of all the people who had come tumbling out of the bar to see the fun, not even any sign of the green. But very dimly I thought I could make out the tops of the two bunkers that flanked the 18th green. It wasn't much to go on, and I could be mistaken – but if I was right, the putting surface must lie between those traps.

Christopher won the toss, casually tossed his ball on to the turf, and with the merest glance over his left shoulder towards the green, swung his nine-iron. The ball soared into the night, and a moment later a cheer went up from behind the green.

There was obviously no way that a mere mortal could hope to compete with this demon of the night, so aiming between what I believed were the two bunkers, I simply allowed the reflexes to take over. My nine-iron swung lazily of its own accord. Even before the roar from behind the green, Dracula had spun round and grasped my hand in congratulation . . . he really *could* see in the dark!

Only when I staggered bemusedly to the edge of the green did I see what had happened. Christopher's ball lay ten feet right of the stick, while mine was only a yard behind, having touched the edge of the hole on its way past.

The nine-iron is one of the most important clubs in 'Mr Lu's' bag too, for this charming little man from Taiwan is one of the world's great short-game players. On the Far East circuit, which next to the American tour is the toughest on which to win consistently, he is the most prolific tournament winner. But before 1971, few of the Asian players had come out of their own part of the world and made the impact their skills deserve in international golf. Mr Lu changed all that at Royal Birkdale, where he harried Lee Trevino and Tony Jacklin right to the last hole of the 1971 Open Championship, and in the process, captured the hearts of the British people. During the four days of the Championship, he managed to convince everybody that he was the world's happiest and most courteous golfer. Every time the gallery applauded him – and there was plenty to applaud in his golf – off would come the little straw hat in a courtly gesture to the crowd to reveal an ear-to-ear grin. Even the most partisan of Jacklin's supporters would have loved to have seen Lu win.

He failed to achieve that victory by a stroke after rounds of 70, 70, 69, 70 – exactly matching Trevino's scores for the last three rounds, but the stocky Mexican who could do no wrong on Birkdale's difficult greens, had opened with a 69. There were many who put Mr Lu's tremendous performance down to the conditions that prevailed on

26　*The gesture that warmed so many hearts at Royal Birkdale. Mr Lu and the famous hat*

this often-stormy Lancashire coast. During this Open, the sun beat down ceaselessly from a cloudless sky, and barely a breath of wind ruffled the flags of the competing nations. Those who suggested that we should never have heard of Lu Liang Huan if conditions had been more 'traditional' for an Open, forget that as long ago as 1964 Lu had achieved a commanding position at the halfway stage of an Open Championship dogged by gales. His midway score of 147 gave him eighth position on the leader board, and he only faded away when weather conditions improved.

At Birkdale seven years later, he was to prove once again that there is more than one way of playing championship-calibre golf, and to give heart to the many other good players who do not possess the fire-power of a Nicklaus or a Weiskopf. Mr Lu hit the ball dead straight, never got himself into trouble, and then shaved strokes from par with his wizardry round the greens.

Most of the best Asian players manufacture their scores in this way, they are all magicians at rolling a potential three strokes into two.

73

27 and 28   Mr Lu – minus hat this time – shows a surprisingly flat top-of-the-swing position on this nine-iron shot

The following week, the little man from Nationalist China travelled across the Channel to play in the French Open over the short Biarritz course. Here was a layout ideally suited to his game, with plenty of short par fours on which he could really make his superb pitching and putting tell. But after the first round, he had absolutely no chance of success. His opening effort of 71 left him no less than seven strokes behind joint leaders Clive Clark and Peter Thomson. Then he really turned on his short-game mastery, with nine-irons and wedges thrown unerringly at the flags, and the putts dropping monotonously into the centre of the cups. His rounds of 63, 62, 66 were good enough to win the title by two strokes from the great Argentinian, Roberto de Vicenzo, and Spain's Vicente Fernandez.

Proving once again that a fine short-game is a match for the most

powerful golf, Lu used his invitation to the Piccadilly World Match-play Championship at the end of the 1971 season. Wentworth in October is one of the longest tests in Europe, but to add to Mr Lu's discomfiture, he had drawn golf's most powerful striker in the first round – Jack Nicklaus. One would have thought that he was hopelessly out-gunned, both by the venue and the opposition. In the end, it was Nicklaus who looked the most uncomfortable, only managing to scramble home on the 35th green. Mr Lu was smiling imperturbably, as usual.

For a normal pitch shot with a nine-iron, Lu sets himself up with a slightly open stance, with the left foot drawn an inch or two back from the orthodox square stance. This automatically throws the club on to a slightly outside-to-in plane and helps to make the backswing steeper. In order to get the ball airborne quickly, and produce maximum stopping power on pitching, Lu tries to keep the backswing steep.

With the ball positioned midway between the feet, he quickly allows the wrists to cock on the backswing, the hands never reaching higher than shoulder-height. The downswing is started by a pronounced pull with the left hand, so that at impact, the clubhead is almost chopping down on to the back of the ball. This steep downswing squeezes the ball out of the turf, producing tremendous backspin.

The follow-through is natural and relaxed, with no great attempt made to keep the hands travelling towards the target once the divot has been taken.

The high-flying pitch is almost entirely a hand and arm swing, with little body movement, but Lu makes sure that his legs are relaxed and his knees unlocked so that his shoulders and hips have the freedom to follow the arm action. And, of course, he keeps his head perfectly still until the ball is flying well on its way towards the target.

Like all great pitchers of the ball, his rhythm is impeccable. He gives the impression of trying to play the shot in slow-motion. There is nothing sloppy about it, the hands are always dominant and in firm control, but both the backswing and downswing are made at a lazy pace – just as if he was trying to pick the ball up on the face of the club and lob it easily at the hole. The distance he hits these shots depends entirely on the length of his backswing, not on the speed of his swing or the effort he puts into his hands at impact – these two factors never vary.

He never attempts to hit a nine-iron hard. Accuracy of striking and accuracy of results are the rewards he is seeking – not power. On the other hand, Lu never falls into the trap that so many handicap golfers do – failing to hit down on the ball sufficiently firmly, which more often than not, is an attempt to 'baby' the pitch shot towards the flag. This so easily leads to topping, or fluffing behind the ball, or any of the faults usual with a sloppy hand action.

Lazy the swing may be, but just as with every other shot he hits, from the drive to the two-foot putt, Lu is concerned with making a crisp and solid contact. Subtlety is no synonym for sloppiness.

When asked during the Birkdale Open what made the Asians the best all-round short-game players in the world, Lu had no hesitation in replying: 'Plactice, plenty a'plactice. We little, not hit ball far, so we gotto plactice.' As he well knows, that kind of practice is not limited to the professionals on the Far East circuit. While the club golfer likes to spend his practice time whooshing his drives down the fairway, all the world's best golfers devote as much as 80 per cent of their practice time to pitching, chipping and putting. They know that the crucial shots round the green are the ones that are going to save their pars when their second shots go astray, or are going to produce the birdies that make the difference between winning and losing a major title.

A good big 'un is nearly always going to beat a good little 'un at the highest level. Nicklaus would be most people's favourite to beat

Lu consistently, despite the little man's devastating short game and the Golden Bear's sometimes suspect work around the greens. But the ability to turn most holes into drives and pitches and to reach the par fives comfortably in two, must tell in the end. At club level, however, this does not apply. A really good short game will defeat even the most powerful of handicap golfers. This department is sadly neglected by the weekend player, yet here is one aspect of the game at which almost anyone – irrespective of size, power or age – can excel.

All you require is plenty a'plactice!

CHAPTER NINE

The Pitching Wedge: Arnold Palmer

No great champion can survive in the maelstrom of top competitive golf without being a supreme wedge player. Since being introduced in the 1930s, this heavy, broad-soled club has done more to bring tournament scores tumbling down than all other factors put together.

So what good reason is there to pick Arnold Palmer as a master wedge player when there are such artists as Gary Player, Weiskopf, Casper or Miller whose superb wedge play help to earn them hundreds of thousands of dollars? The answer lies in the fact that Palmer's ability with this club, if not underrated, was certainly unrecognized when he was golf's undisputed super-star.

One of the great attractions for the world-wide battalions of Arnie's Army was that he was always liable to produce the unexpected. His last round 'charges' became famous when he made up seemingly impossible ground during the last 18 holes to snatch major titles. Just as famous, and exciting for the crowds, was his penchant for hitting drives into such deep trouble that only the combined searching power of the Army could find the ball. Then he would extricate himself dramatically, and pitch and putt to rescue his par. These became sensational trademarks, but while galleries gasped at his fairway-eating drives, or thrilled to his miraculous recovery shots, they tended to overlook the shot that ultimately produced most birdies, or saved most pars – the wedge to the green.

In 1960 Palmer had been a professional for six years. He had already won one of golf's major titles, the 1958 Masters at Augusta, but during those half-dozen years he admitted that he was still learning his trade, still struggling to cope with the pressure that every tournament golfer feels to some extent. In 1960 he was to change the world's attitudes to the game, encourage millions to take up golf by example, and to prove himself the dominant figure of his age.

The year started for him at Augusta in April, at the fabulous Masters tournament. He had played brilliantly on the winter section of the Tour, winning four tournaments, and by the time he arrived in Georgia he was brimful of confidence.

In the first round he completed Augusta in 67, an effort that shot him into the lead from which he was never displaced. This was a fine round, made special by his immaculate wedge play and putting,

29 At his peak, Palmer often found himself in this kind of situation, and relied on his wedge to get him out of trouble. Now he tends to hit the ball straighter

without which it might easily have been only a par round. During the two middle rounds his putting touch deserted him. His scores of 73 and 72 left him in front, but his nearest challengers, Dow Finsterwald and Ken Venturi were too close for comfort. In fact, had Finsterwald not been penalized two strokes in the first round for taking a practice putt after completing one of the holes, he would have led by a stroke going into the final round.

Over the back nine on that final day, Palmer was evidently feeling the pressure of his slender lead. At hole after hole, his second shots missed the greens, and only his pitching wedge saved him. Repeatedly he popped the ball up close, and the putter that had given him trouble in the previous two rounds, came to his rescue again. By the time he came to the 14th, he learned that Venturi had completed the tournament with a 70 for a total of 283, while Finsterwald had finished with 71 to total a stroke more. That meant he needed a birdie in the last four holes to tie Venturi, and two birdies to win outright.

The 17th at Augusta is 400 yards long. Needing to go for everything now, Palmer cut loose with his driver to the utter disbelief of the packed gallery that tightly encircled the hole. So long was his drive, that he was able to hit a pitching wedge for his second shot, and a few moments later his putt had curled into the hole. Now with the adrenalin really pulsing through him, he hit a six-iron to within five feet at the 420-yard 18th, and in went that one to give him a 70, and victory by one stroke. The legend of the Palmer 'charge' was repeated.

The most dramatic charge of Palmer's career came only a couple of months later. The US Open was played at Cherry Hills, near Denver, that year, but any thoughts that Palmer might have had of collecting this title must have faded after his first three rounds. He had started 72, 71, 72 for a 54-holes score of 215. The lead was held by the burly Mike Souchak at 208, seven strokes clear of Palmer, while among the phalanx of players also ahead of him were such names as Nicklaus, Player, Hogan, Finsterwald, Boros, Casper and Sam Snead – a real roll of honour!

However, Palmer has never been a quitter, and from the moment he stepped on to the first tee for the last round, he was still trying to win the national Open. The first hole at Cherry Hills is only 350 yards, but a belt of rough extends across the fairway short of the green to prevent it being reached by long hitters. Palmer lashed into his drive, as only he can, and the ball bounded through the long grass and on to the heart of the green. Two putts gave him the first birdie in what was to prove one of the most dramatic rounds ever played.

At the 2nd, he missed the green, but holed out with his wedge for another birdie. The third is similar in length to the opening hole, but this time another enormous drive drew away to the left of the putting surface. Another delicate pitch with the wedge almost went into the hole for an eagle. When he holed a long putt at the 4th, Palmer had started the long haul back with four straight birdies. Two more came at the 6th and 7th, and finally he reached the turn in 30 of the most devastating strokes the US Open had ever seen. Suddenly, there were seven players, including Palmer, tying for the lead, and when he hit a four-iron into the heart of the long 11th and two-putted for his seventh birdie, his nose was in front for the first time.

What followed was almost anti-climax, for the 'best' he could do was to par the remaining seven holes. Yet, there was still one vital moment to come. Playing the 18th, Palmer's main rivals were still behind him on the course, and he was not to know whether they would be able to make up his slender lead – every shot still counted, every shot was crucial.

The 18th at Cherry Hills measures 468 yards over a large lake. This time, Palmer's four-iron carried left of the green into fringe rough. Once more, his brilliant wedge play saved the situation. A delicate pitch-and-run left him less than a yard from the hole, and in went the putt for an almost miraculous 65. This round stood as a record for the final 18 in the Open until Miller's similarly inspired 63 at Oakmont in 1973. In the end, Palmer's winning margin was two shots, with the amateur Nicklaus finishing at 282. The following year Nicklaus – by then a professional – was to have his revenge by defeating Palmer in an 18-hole play-off for the title.

With both the Masters and the US Open tucked safely under his belt, and Palmer at the height of his magnificent powers, the Grand Slam of the four major world championships in the same year was now a realistic possibility. He crossed the Atlantic to play in the British Open for the first time.

The 1960 Open was special, for it was precisely a hundred years since Willie Park had taken the first title from seven other competitors with a 36-hole total of 174 at Prestwick. Palmer's presence this time made the event even more special, for here, in the flesh, was the sporting legend of the age who had hitherto only been seen on film by the British fans. There never was a hotter favourite to take the title in the long history of the world's oldest Championship. Where else could this particular event be played but at the Home of Golf, St Andrews?

At the halfway stage, Palmer was struggling with the alien conditions – although after his electrifying charge at Denver we still believed him to be capable of anything. Roberto de Vicenzo, the much-loved Argentinian, had started brilliantly with two rounds of 67, for 134; Kel Nagle, a charming Australian then in his fortieth year, was two strokes behind after rounds of 69 and 67; then came Palmer (70, 71) and Peter Thomson (72, 69) on 141. Thomson had already won the Open four times, and was to win again at Royal Birkdale five years later.

In the third round, both de Vicenzo and Thomson struggled to 75s, which ended the Australian's challenge this time, but kept the Argentinian still well in the hunt. Palmer's 70 had closed the gap on the leader to four strokes – Nagle 207, de Vicenzo 209, Palmer 211. *Now*, we said to ourselves, there will be no holding him.

30 and 31   Still one of the most exhilarating power swings in the game. Arnold Palmer in full cry with a big iron

Nor did Palmer disappoint us. All the last round brilliance was there; the famous charge was in operation. However, in the final event, his 68 was not quite good enough – Nagle hung on grimly under immense psychological pressure over the final few holes, and his total of 278 was good enough to take the Centenary Open by one stroke from the great American. Nor was Palmer to win the US PGA Championship that year, and that tournament remains the one outstanding title he has failed to win during his incredible career.

In the Masters, the American Open and the Open at St Andrews, Palmer's work on and around the greens was the most important feature of his play; the quality of his wedge play had certainly been the deciding factor at Denver.

Since his fortieth birthday in 1969, Palmer has hit the ball more consistently than when at his peak in the early 1960s. With advancing years, the powerhouse has slowed down a little, and while he hits the ball only a little less far than in his heyday, his quieter swing has eradicated the occasional wild shot that used to beset him at critical moments. Today, he is possibly less dependent on his wedge than at any other time in his career, simply because he hits more greens in regulation figures. The facet of his game that has declined, although not to the extent that he likes to believe, is his putting. If he had retained the ability to charge long putts into the hole, he would still be winning major titles consistently.

As with every other area of his game, Palmer's play round the greens was naturally aggressive when he ruled the golf roost. This aggression is as inherent in his wedge swing as it is from the tee. He rarely leaves a pitch shot short of the hole because his technique is founded on firmness, crispness of stroke and, above all, confidence. It is very much a 'hand' technique, with the left hand and wrist predominating. Except on occasions where he needs to play a particularly high-flying wedge, Palmer tends to play a push-shot, with the left wrist remaining relatively firm throughout the stroke.

From a narrow, open stance, with the knees well flexed, he pushes the club back with his left hand, allowing the wrists to 'give' naturally rather than making any conscious effort to cock them. The left hand controls the downswing, pulling the blade of the club into the back of the ball, and through the impact area, so that the hands are leading when contact is made.

Even on the longest wedge shots, his hands are never taken further back than shoulder-height, although naturally, there is a greater degree of wrist cock.

As with all short shots around the green, the tempo of the swing is the most important factor. Many great players seem to swing the club more slowly than Palmer, but he only appears to be faster because he insists on firmness throughout the stroke, which helps him to produce maximum backspin on the ball. However, there is no suggestion of any speeding up in the impact area – the swing is completed at an even speed, with the hands firmly in control throughout.

With the broad-soled wedge it is more important than with any other club to make an accurate contact, striking the ball first and then taking a divot. This accounts for Palmer's weight distribution throughout the stroke, which is concentrated on his left side. This, combined with a hand action that leads the clubhead into the ball, guarantees him an arc *down* into the back of the ball, producing the ball/turf sequence.

Confidence is the overriding factor of successful wedge play. Long hours of practice and continual use under pressure develops in players like Palmer an intimate relationship with the pitching wedge that club golfers rarely achieve. Partly for this reason, and partly because the Americans regularly play to well-watered greens, the top golfers often use their wedges for shots too tricky for the weekend golfer to risk.

Because his judgement is good, Palmer will often play a shot from just off the putting surface with a wedge, having selected the right spot on which the ball shall pitch, and having estimated carefully the degree of backspin he can apply from that particular lie. This is pin-point golf, where the margin for error is very slight. He would be sure to advise weekend golfers in similar circumstances to play a more straight-faced club and to roll the ball at the hole with an ordinary chip shot.

With practice, however, and the resultant confidence, the handicap player can save innumerable strokes with his wedge, and it is well worth spending time experimenting with shots for special occasions – the cut-up shot, for instance, which can be invaluable for getting the ball quickly into the air over an intervening bunker. Most people will be surprised at the versatility that can be achieved with this club, merely by altering the set-up position slightly, or by using varying degrees of wrist action.

When Arnold Palmer first emerged as a world-class player in the late 1950s, he had his critics. The most common criticism was that an action which depended so much on pure physical strength could not possibly endure, and that Palmer's reign at the top must surely be strictly limited. What those critics possibly failed to take into account was the personality of the man. So strong is his competitive urge, so uninhibited is his pleasure in winning, that he has more than made up for any shortcomings in technique.

While it is true that he has not won any of the Big Four championships since his 1964 Masters title, Palmer's play is still of the highest championship calibre. Despite his in-built desire to knock the cover off the ball, he has made the concession to advancing years, and now that his swing is so much less dependent on strength, he hits the ball from tee to green with a greater consistency than he ever achieved at his peak.

It may also be true that today's super-stars – Miller, Weiskopf and Nicklaus – and the budding super-stars of tomorrow have more reliable and enduring actions than Arnold Palmer. But anyone who suggests that in the late 1970s the first great champion of the modern era is nothing but a has-been, has only to watch him when he is playing well in a major tournament, and notice the ecstatic reactions of the still-faithful Army who have memories that go back to Palmer's palmy days.

Golf has been kind to Palmer; the game has made him a dollar multi-millionaire. But he has given a tremendous amount back in terms of pleasure and in bringing about a sociological change in the very foundations of the sport. Only a really great champion, and an even greater personality, can do that.

*32   Unquestionably, Gary Player is the best in the world at extricating himself
from the greenside bunkers without conceding a shot to par*

CHAPTER TEN

Bunker Shots: Gary Player

When Gary Player was learning his trade as a young man in South Africa, he made a fetish of practice that has remained with him ever since. Every day, from dawn to dusk, he hit shots on the golf course until his hands bled, and he thought his diminutive frame could stand no more.

Such practice sessions convinced him that he must concentrate on physical fitness if he ever hoped to compete on equal terms with the great champions of the time. His physical training sessions are as much a daily routine now as they were twenty years ago. The two regimens of his life – practice and fitness – have kept him one of golf's super-stars since the day he earned international fame by winning the Open Championship at Muirfield in 1959.

33   A study in competitive determination – the greatest individual factor in Gary Player's climb to superstardom

34   *Notice how Player has driven the hands through sand and ball, but is not in a position to continue into a fuller follow-through position*

In those early days of raw fingers and unceasing endeavour, he was not to know of the fame and riches that lay before him. He likes to tell the story of those all-day practice sessions, and recalls that he would always end up by playing bunker shots from a greenside trap. His personal rule was that he would not go home to his dinner until he had holed out at least three times from the sand. On and on he would go, ignoring hunger and darkness until he had achieved his object. That is the way he has lived his entire life, by stating an objective and working tirelessly until it has been achieved.

Defining the facets of his game that have made Player a super-star is difficult. His long game is good enough, but not outstanding. He seems unprepared to accept his lack of stature, and from time to time attempts to force the longer clubs in order to hit as far as Nicklaus. The usual result is a hook. His iron shots are sound, but no better than those of many other professionals; certainly not so superior that they can make up his deficiencies from the tee.

Near the greens, Player is the absolute master – possibly the finest 'touch' golfer in the world today. He has no peers when it comes to pitching and chipping, and he is unarguably one of the two best putters from eight feet. Only Bob Charles, playing his best, holes out as many at this crucial length.

If at times Player wondered in the gloom of a South African sunset, while his evening meal was getting cold, whether it was all worth-while, he can now reflect that those long hours spent hitting out of bunkers have helped him to earn millions of dollars and become one of only four men to win the Open Championships of Britain and America, the Masters and the US PGA Championship – the golf world's four great titles. When one considers the other three are Nicklaus, Ben Hogan and Gene Sarazen, then one starts to appreciate just how great a golfer Player is.

Unquestionably, Gary Player is the best in the world at extricating himself from greenside bunkers without conceding a shot to par. He seems to have an understanding for the 'feel' of sand, and the ability to calculate exactly just what effects a particular grade of sand will have on the clubface.

It is, of course, no more than practice and experience, plus the common sense to make himself thoroughly aware of the texture of the sand before a tournament starts, yet the way in which he splashes the ball out to within a foot or two of the hole is uncanny.

One rarely associates bunker play with championship-winning performances, yet I can think of one or two instances where supreme shots with the sand wedge have saved the situation. Over the second nine holes of his third round at Royal Lytham in 1969, Tony Jacklin seemed to put himself into every available greenside bunker. Yet at hole after hole he splashed out and knocked the ensuing putt into the cup to hold his score together. The following day he took the Open title.

For Player, there may have been more dramatic occasions when his bunker shots have brought him rich titles, but the one that sticks

*35 Jacklin at Lytham in 1969. His bunker play in the third round left him in
a position to win the Open the next day*

in everyone's mind was the final of the Piccadilly World Match-play Championship at Wentworth in 1973. In truth, it has to be said that Graham Marsh, the immensely talented Australian, played the better golf, particularly over the four extra holes played in the deepening gloom of an October evening. Three times in those four holes Player was bunkered, and each time he was down in two. In fact, he made a birdie four from sand at the 40th hole to take the title when Marsh three-putted.

What has made Player the best bunker player in the world is an absolute confidence in his method, and an iron determination which keeps him trying when all is apparently going wrong. Indeed, this competitive determination, above all else, is probably the factor that helped him to achieve super-stardom.

The modern sand wedge has made most normal bunker shots as straightforward as an ordinary pitch shot. Still, the club golfer tends to be gripped by panic when he sees his ball heading for the sand. One suspects that it is not the innate problems of the hazard that cause this degree of mental stress, but simply the realization that he has not been in a bunker for the past month, and can he remember how the shot should be played?

I am sure this is the key to the weekend player's worries: he is suddenly confronted with a set of problems that occur relatively infrequently in the course of several rounds of golf, and he has not made any effort to practise and develop a technique to cope with those problems. With such indecision and nervousness, it is hardly surprising that fears are justified by his results more often than not. A little time occasionally spent knocking balls from the practice bunker would be more than sufficient to give the player at least an inkling of what he is trying to do, and the basis of a sound method.

The most commonly used bunker shot from a greenside trap where the ball is lying reasonably well is the standard splash shot. The object is for the sole of the sand wedge to splash into the sand an inch or so behind the ball, travel just under the surface and almost lift the ball out on a cushion of sand. The broad, rounded sole of the purpose-built club guarantees that it does not dig too deep, but almost bounces through the top layer of sand. At this shot Player excels.

He sets himself up with a very open stance, with knees well flexed and pointing slightly towards the target. This means that his weight is concentrated on the right foot to ensure that the club bounces through the sand rather than burying itself under the ball. Player is particularly choosey about his footing in a bunker, and usually spends some time shuffling his feet into the sand so that he eliminates all risk of slipping.

How far behind the ball he addresses – the spot where he wants the club to hit the sand – depends entirely on the texture. In firm, heavy sand it may be as much as two inches behind the ball, but in the soft, powdery sand of our seaside courses, it could be half that distance. Soft, fine sand dissipates clubhead speed much more effectively than heavy inland sand. The important thing is that once he has decided how far behind the ball the clubhead must enter, he focuses his entire attention *on that spot,* and not on the ball.

The swing is made with the hands and arms only, with the wrists cocking almost immediately on the backswing. This steep arc is guaranteed to lift the ball quickly over the face of the bunker. Still concentrating on the spot behind the ball, Player pulls the clubhead down towards the ball with both hands, without making any conscious attempt to uncock the wrists. This steep, downward swing at the ball ensures that his wedge hits the sand behind and continues in a shallow arc under the ball.

Player does not attempt much follow-through on these shots, but makes certain that the clubhead goes right through sand and ball.

The most noticeable thing about every top-class bunker player is the slow rhythm with which he executes the stroke. The length of the shot is not dictated by the speed or effort put into the swing, but simply by the length of the backswing. Player swings his sand wedge very slowly back and not appreciably faster on the downswing, meanwhile riveting his eyes on the spot where he wants the club to enter the sand.

Everyone agrees that the most important feature of consistent bunker play is to keep the head still, but the logic of that particular advice becomes the more apparent when one appreciates that unless you concentrate on the point of entry, you risk losing control and accuracy. For the further benefit of the club golfer with misgivings when he is in sand, such concentration leaves no room in the mind for fears of failure.

In an ideal world, every time your ball goes into a bunker you should find it resting on a smooth and well-raked piece of sand. Unfortunately, this does not always happen, and there are occasions when you find yourself resting in a heel-print, or faced with a ball half-plugged in soft sand.

In such bad lies, Player makes a couple of important alterations to his set-up position. Rather than playing the ball from the middle of his feet, as in the conventional splash shot, he addresses it rather more towards the right foot. Also, he concentrates his weight on the left leg, for his intention now is to hit down hard behind the ball without attempting to force the clubhead through the cushion of sand.

With the face of his wedge hooded, so that the resistance of the broad sole is minimized, he aims to hit about an inch behind the ball, and drive the clubhead deep into the sand. In a bad lie such as this, he often elects to use a pitching wedge rather than a sand wedge because its sharper leading edge bites deeper into the sand. It is surprising how hard he can hit this shot, and yet the ball only pops gently over the lip of the bunker, the power having been dissipated in the bunker.

Confidence, or rather the lack of it, is the only thing that separates most club players from successful bunker play. Yet this confidence is easy to acquire if one takes time when playing from sand; one learns by experience how club and ball will react from different textures.

If golf is supposed to be played for fun, why live with a shot that terrifies?

36 Lee Trevino and a winning smile

CHAPTER ELEVEN

The Champion Scrambler: Lee Trevino

There never was an Open like Muirfield 1972. And the 85,000 people who were there, as well as the countless millions all over the world who watched it on television, would probably say that there never will be another like it. For although the Royal and Ancient Golf Club, those tournament organizers supreme, can continue to mix the same ingredients, it seems almost inconceivable that the cake could ever turn out like this one.

Muirfield had everything. There was Nicklaus, who arrived in Scotland bestriding the game like a colossus. He was stretching for what had been believed to be an unattainable star, but now here he was, winner in 1972 of the Masters and the US Open, needing to win the Open and the US PGA Championship to complete the modern Grand Slam of the world's four classic titles in one year. He maintained that the idea of the Grand Slam was merely a concoction of the press, but with two down and two to go, he was obviously giving all of himself to achieving the impossible dream. By the time this Open was over, nobody could deny that it could be done, and even more remarkably that there were two men capable of doing it.

Nicklaus did not win the Open. For three days he had little idea where his iron shots were going, largely, one suspects, as a direct result of his uncharacteristic defensive strategy. This strategy was forced upon him by the golf course, rather than any other problem.

Muirfield is one of the world's great seaside tests, but during this July week it lay shimmering in the soft heat haze beside the Firth of Forth, its fangs apparently drawn. But, there were other problems. The putting surfaces were green oases amid a brown desert of short linksland turf; the wind was not to blow during the Championship, but Muirfield was to show all the subtleties of a fast-running seaside course in high summer.

Then there was Trevino. He had won the Open at Royal Birkdale the previous year, climaxing perhaps the most incredible three weeks in golf history. In the first week he had won the American Open, beating Nicklaus in an 18-hole play-off; then he had travelled directly to Montreal, where he beat Art Wall in a sudden-death play-off for the Canadian Open; and then straight to Birkdale, where he managed to fend off the close attentions of the delightful little man from Taiwan, Lu Liang Huan.

Trevino came to Muirfield to defend his Open title with a successful campaign on the American circuit behind him, but without having

95

featured to any great degree in the Nicklaus bonanza of the major championships.

Then there was another aspect that the Royal and Ancient could not have planned. Tony Jacklin stood on the first tee on Wednesday, made a smooth and rhythmic swing, and crashed the ball straight up the narrow fairway. From that moment we knew he was playing well; one can always see what kind of form he is in by watching the tempo of his swing.

This was the largest crowd ever to attend an Open. They were to be kept at fever pitch for the entire four days of the championship as one drama followed another. They, more than any single factor, created an atmosphere of such electricity that this championship had a personality all its own.

The excitement mounted from the outset, with Jacklin taking an immediate lead over the other main contenders after a round of 69, and then being joined at the head of the list by the defending champion after two rounds. Although at the time it bore no particular portent, Trevino had holed a chip to help him on his way to the joint lead.

At the halfway stage, Muirfield's leader board read rather like golf's Who's Who:

141 – Tony Jacklin 69, 72
Lee Trevino 71, 70
142 – Jack Nicklaus 70, 72
Doug Sanders 71, 71
Gary Player 71, 71
Peter Townsend 70, 72
Johnny Miller 76, 66
John Garner 71, 71

Doug Sanders, so beloved by the Scottish crowds after his tragedy of two years earlier when only a yard of St Andrews turf on the final green stood between him and the Open, had been in a position to spreadeagle the field, but over the closing holes in each round, disaster overtook him. Though he continued to play well for the rest of the championship, ultimately finishing fourth, the title he has vowed to win had eluded him for another year.

The other round that the fans went scurrying to watch was Johnny Miller's 66 – just ten strokes better than his opening effort. Miller was making his debut as a professional in Britain, and we were not to know then that less than a year later we would be shaking our heads in disbelief at one of the most remarkable rounds of golf ever played – Miller's 63 in the final round of the American Open.

Muirfield 1972 bubbled for the first two days and really exploded on the third day. Jack Nicklaus, still a hot favourite for the title, shot 71. On any other day, that would have been good enough to have kept him firmly in the hunt. But on this day it left him trailing Trevino by six strokes, an apparently hopeless margin with only a round to go. However, the Nicklaus story was not quite over. In the last round, he set a mental target of 65 to give himself a chance of the title. Suddenly he was back to his imperious best. He stormed through, failing by only one stroke to continue the Grand Slam dream, and he left Muirfield with his reputation as the world's best not only intact, but enhanced. A birdie at the 17th hole would have given him his 65, and a tie for the championship.

In hindsight, one can only wonder by how many shots he might have won the title if only he had treated the great course with a little less respect for the first three days, and had been prepared to bully it a little more. Unlike players such as Peter Thomson and Doug Sanders, Nicklaus's game is not based on subtlety. He admits that he finds difficulty in manoeuvring the ball one way and then the other. His great weapons are power and precision striking. For most of this Open, he muzzled his cannon, and his chance of the Grand Slam was gone.

From the halfway point, the Open Championship belonged to the two leaders, Jacklin and Trevino. Jacklin was playing better than when he had won the title at Royal Lytham three years earlier, and his playing partner, Trevino, was reaching within himself to clutch at a source of inspiration that perhaps even he did not know existed.

Over the last nine holes of that third round they traded birdies in almost unbelievable fashion. Like two well-matched boxers, they countered each other's body blows with cold precision. It was more than the most hardened observer could stand, and the often-reticent Scottish spectators were almost driven to hysteria.

Trevino birdied the 14th and 15th, but at the short 16th he was bunkered beside the green. His trap-shot was too hard, but it hit the flag halfway up and dropped down, straight into the hole. A fluke? Well, lucky anyway. . . . His fourth successive birdie came at the long 17th, a hole on which fortunes were to swing and history to be made the following day. So they came to the difficult par-four 18th, still level after 53 holes, and both needing pars for 67s. Jacklin's second shot found the heart of the green, and his four was a formality. But Trevino's aggressive stroke had run through the back of the green into some short, hairy rough. A moment or two later he was dancing a Mexican jig as his chip shot rolled down the lightning-fast green and dropped gently into the hole. A 66 and a one-stroke lead for the defending champion.

If the dramas of the previous evening had been more than anyone could bear, Saturday was worse. Another glorious day, with cloudless blue skies and the Firth of Forth shimmering in the sunlight. The champagne tent doing record business while the early starters go through the motions of completing the championship. As the time approaches for Jacklin and Trevino to restart their absorbing battle, the champagne tent magically empties.

To the uninhibited delight of the patriots, Jacklin holds firm, still matching Trevino stroke for stroke. He has regained the one-stroke deficit with which he started the last day, and as the round draws towards its inexorable climax, news filters back of Nicklaus's phenomenal effort. His 66 has given him a total of 279, and the spectre of the Grand Slam again flickers briefly.

But as Jacklin and Trevino stand on the 17th tee, they know that two pars will give them totals of 278 to beat Nicklaus. In these gentle conditions the Golden Bear had made the costly mistake of failing to birdie this hole, and its importance is now crucial to the two leading protagonists. A birdie here from either could settle their personal battle.

One can only guess at Jacklin's feelings of relief when Trevino's drive went into deep, clinging rough. He could only chop his ball back on to the fairway. Still short of the green in three, his fourth scuttled across the putting surface, finishing in the light rough over the back in four. The scene was set for one of the cruellest dramas ever to take place in a championship. Jacklin, little more than twenty paces short of the flag in two – and looking for a birdie – played a delicate pitch-and-run which checked unaccountably on the fast green. Instead of running close to the hole, the ball stopped fifteen feet short. A disappointment for Jacklin, perhaps, but nothing to worry about, for surely he must play the last with at least one stroke in hand. . . .

What happened next is best described in Trevino's own words as he told it to the press corps afterwards: 'As I walked up to my ball, I knew I'd lost the Open. I didn't take much notice of what I was doing, just walked up, hit it, and it went in the hole.' Just like that.

Jacklin said later: 'From that moment, I didn't know what I was doing. I completed that hole and the 18th in a daze.' In his daze, he three-putted the 17th to fall a stroke behind, and the fact that he took five at the 18th is academic, apart from the fact that it allowed Nicklaus's 279 total to slip into clear second place. Trevino, of course, reprieved and with the adrenalin coursing through his veins, never faltered, and at the last came within a whisker of a birdie three.

What can one say about a man who always seems capable of producing blinding inspiration just at the moment when most needed? No doubt many will point to the four crucial occasions when he holed from off the green during this championship, and put his win down to great good fortune. That would be less than fair, for lucky though he undoubtedly was, it gives no credit for the other great shots he played over four days, the pressure putts he holed to keep himself in contention, the skilful flighting of the ball into firm, fast greens.

Those four shots were the difference between winning and losing the championship, and while Trevino may be regarded as fortunate that they all went into the hole, one should remember that a great deal of his success depends on his scrambling around the greens. At Royal Birkdale in 1971 he achieved victory not by superior striking, but by consistently getting down in two from off the green. Many a competitor at Troon in 1973 must have muttered 'here we go again' when he chipped into the hole at the 18th to complete his first round.

The difference between lipping the hole and dropping is fractional, and dependent on good fortune. Equally inescapable is the fact that if a man can consistently put the ball very close to the hole, he increases the percentages of chance. Trevino is a master at rolling three shots into two, and this facility does not seem to desert him even when he is not playing his best. This is what makes Trevino golf's champion scrambler.

Scrambling is not dependent on first-class technique. Indeed, almost by definition, it is the art of manufacturing a shot to fit the circumstances – and this often means making an unorthodox stroke. Trevino's great assets are: a wonderful feeling of touch, in other words, almost perfect judgement of pace; and the imagination to visualize the most effective stroke. He believes that any iron club, from two-iron to sand wedge, can be used for scrambling near the green.

The basics of a good chipping technique must be learnt if you are to have the confidence to strike the ball correctly and judge the lie of the land. Of even greater value are imagination and judgement. These are not heaven-sent gifts. They can be learnt through constant usage and regular practice – which is perhaps why Trevino, in common with all the other top professionals, spends so much time practising the little shots and his short-range putting. One must never forget that there is no earthly use in acquiring the necessary skills for consistently scrambling the ball within three or four feet of the hole if you then make only half the putts. The putt is 50 per cent of 'getting down in two'.

Scrambling should have particular attractions for the handicap golfer. Not only is this shot golf's most important stroke-saver, but it is less dependent on striking ability than any other department of the game, and age is no barrier to good stroke-saving.

Trevino's Method

As the chip shot, where the ball is allowed to run across the surface of the green for most of the distance, is the fundamental stroke in the scrambler's armoury, Trevino's chipping action is worth studying.

The essence is that he strikes the right balance between relaxation and crispness. There is no sloppiness about Trevino's action, nor is there any suggestion of a quick jab at the ball.

His set-up position is simple and comfortable. The feet are close together, only a few inches apart, and he stands fairly tall to the ball. By standing up, he brings the ball close to his feet so that there is no suggestion of reaching out with the hands; and his eyes are fairly well over the ball.

The ball positioning, in relation to the feet, varies an inch or two depending on the club that Trevino is using and the kind of shot he wants to play. If he wants to keep the ball low by hooding the club-face, producing backspin on the bounce, then the ball is placed just inside the right toe. In fact, this was the method he used at Muirfield's 71st hole when he used a wedge so that the ball checked on the fast green before rolling gently across the turf to the hole.

On the other hand, if he must get the ball up quickly over a hump

37 and 38   The extraordinary scything swing of Lee Trevino: highly individual, and highly effective

to a flag where there is a lot of intervening green, then he plays the ball just forward of centre, so that contact is made fractionally on the upswing and there is little backspin on pitching.

Trevino concentrates his weight on the left leg, so that he achieves a slightly descending blow giving the important ball/turf sequence so vital to all iron shots. He also tends to grip the club an inch or two down the shaft so that his hands are in closer contact with the clubhead, giving him a greater sense of feel and control.

The swing is made with the hands and arms alone, with just a little 'give' in the knees to keep it smooth and relaxed. There is no body movement as such, but the action is sufficiently 'unlocked' to follow

the action of the hands. Freedom from muscular tension is one of the great keys to good chipping.

The left hand predominates throughout this little swing, pushing the clubhead back low to the ground, and then pulling in towards the ball and through the impact area. There is no deliberate wrist action, but neither is there a conscious effort to keep the wrists stiff – they 'give' a little without breaking. With the back of the left hand facing the hole and dominating the stroke, Trevino makes contact with the hands fractionally ahead of the ball. This gives him lift, spin, an accurate strike at the back of the ball and control. As always, his head remains perfectly still throughout the stroke. Even at Muirfield, when it apparently did not matter and he 'just walked up an' hit it', Lee Trevino did not break that basic law of golf.

As has been said elsewhere in this book, the best-equipped strikers do not necessarily become the super-star champions. Actually, Trevino is one of the best and one of the most skilful manoeuvrers of a golf ball on the long shots, despite his raking unorthodox swing. Nevertheless, his ability to charm the ball close to the hole and then unfailingly hole out has taken him from the ranks of good golfers and elevated him to the very top.

39   This is the kind of shot where Trevino is lethal, and where championships are won and lost − as Jacklin knows to his cost

40 Bob Charles, who has proved that putting is not a matter of luck. It is as much a golf shot as the drive or five-iron

The Champion Putter : Bob Charles

At the highest level of competition there is little to choose between the world's best golfers. All drive well, play their second shots accurately and reduce pitching to an apparently facile art. Nevertheless, the man who wins the championship is the man who holes most putts.

Everyone is capable of putting brilliantly, from the lowliest of club players upwards, but at champion standard the great players have more brilliant putting days. Certainly, many major events have been won by brilliance on the greens. The outstanding record was Bert Yancey's total of 102 putts in the 72 holes of the 1966 Portland Open.

Among the consistently *good* putters, rather than the occasionally brilliant ones, we find the world's best. Even among the world's great players, there are some who stand out on the putting green. How many more championships might Nicklaus have won if he had consistently holed the six-footers that Gary Player never seems to miss?

Player is certainly one of the great putters, and so too are Billy Casper, Tom Weiskopf and Lee Trevino, all of whom have proved under intense pressure their ability to hole the vital putts.

But above them all I have to rank the lanky New Zealand left-hander, Bob Charles – possibly the only man in golf who has never moaned about his putting stroke! I trust that I am not being unfair or unkind when I say that Bob's game from tee to green has made him into a good golfer, but his ability on the greens has made him great.

Prior to the 1963 Open Championship, at Royal Lytham and St Annes, Charles was recognized only as the world's best left-handed golfer. After winning the title, he established himself as one of the international elite who is a champion in any company.

At the halfway stage of the 1963 Open, the field was led by a short and stocky extrovert from the United States, Phil Rodgers. He had been among the first of the American circuit players to follow Palmer's lead by crossing the Atlantic for the Open, and the previous year had tied for third place behind Palmer – although it has to be said he was thirteen strokes behind.

But at Lytham, which has produced some of the Open's lowest scores, he started as if fired from a gun. Rounds of 67 and 68 left him a stroke ahead of the inevitable Peter Thomson, three ahead of Nicklaus and four clear of Kel Nagle. Bob Charles had started well with a 68, but had slipped to 72 to be five strokes adrift at halfway.

The situation changed dramatically in the third round as Charles continued to play his steady rather than inspirational brand of golf, but putt after putt dropped on the beautifully true Lytham greens. His round of 66, the best of the tournament, carried him into a one-stroke lead over Thomson, with Nicklaus and Rodgers a further stroke behind.

At the climax of the championship, Nicklaus had every chance to win, but at the last two holes he hit poor chips from just off the green, and failed to get either of the putts in. And so it was to be decided by the final pair on the course, Charles and Rodgers. The chunky American had been playing well, while Charles had been holding his game together with some ice-cool putting, without which the two Americans would have been fighting for the title.

And so they came to the last hole, Rodgers needing par for a 69, Charles for a 71. Rodgers coaxed in his putt from six feet, and in his elation, threw his hat over the hole and indulged in some light-hearted histrionics. It did not affect Charles in the slightest, and when both Rodgers and the crowd had calmed down, he rolled his four-footer into the centre of the cup for a tie at 277, one ahead of Nicklaus.

At that time, the play-off was over 36 holes the following day, and from the point of view of excitement, it proved to be anticlimactic. Even in its earliest stages, it became clear that the New Zealander's putting would prove the decisive factor. At the end of the day he had totalled 140 against Rodgers' 148, and the American could only remark ruefully: 'He putted me straight off the golf course.'

From the moment that he was presented with the Open Championship trophy, Charles increased dramatically in international stature. He became a big money-winner on the American circuit, and apart from winning several run-of-the-mill US tournaments, he collected the 1968 Canadian Open, and the Piccadilly World Match-play Championship the following year.

But never was his putting a more valuable weapon than during two weeks of October 1972. The John Player Classic tournament was played for the first time at the magnificent Turnberry course on the Ayrshire coast, offering over £56,000 to thirty-one top professionals who had qualified from the world's major circuits. Apart from the British spearhead of Jacklin and Peter Oosterhuis, there were such players as Palmer, Doug Sanders, Gay Brewer, Billy Casper, Roberto de Vicenzo, Tom Weiskopf and Gary Player in the field. Indeed, after a relatively quiet year, Charles must have considered himself fortunate to be included in this elite company as a result of his performances on the New Zealand circuit.

However, grabbing his chance, Charles played impeccably for the first three rounds, continually getting down in a chip and a putt on many of Turnberry's most fearsome holes. When the gale blew up on the final day, so strongly that Gary Player was blown to an 85 and the exciting Jerry Heard to 86, Charles maintained his steadiness from tee to green, and more important, his putting stroke did not fail him even in these difficult conditions. He won the £15,000 first

41   An unusual show of emotion from Bob Charles, who finds nothing extraordinary in holing every putt! This one went in . . . of course

*42   In Charles's putting stroke, the shoulders and arms form a triangle that
remains constant throughout the stroke. He pushes the ball towards the hole by a
rocking action of the shoulders*

prize by one stroke from Oosterhuis and Brewer.

The following week he competed in the Dunlop Masters tournament at Newcastle, and after a tremendous dogfight the whole way
with Tony Jacklin, he grabbed the title and a further £2,000. Jacklin
had led the tournament for 67 holes, but at the crucial moment his
putting betrayed him. Charles on the other hand, completed his
second successive tournament without once three-putting.

Now that he has given up playing the American circuit and concentrates on the British and European events, Charles has become one
of the most feared competitors this side of the Atlantic. He quit the

United States because, he said, he simply had not enough power from the tee to compete against the majority of the players on the circuit.

I suspect, too, that he found his greatest weapon, his putting, did not gain its full reward on American courses. It is interesting that he always putts well in Britain, particularly on fast seaside greens, and it should be remembered that generally the turf on European greens is of a much finer and less variable texture than is found on the majority of American courses.

Charles's pendulum putting action which *rolls* the ball smoothly towards the hole, is ideal for fast greens, but is unlikely to work as effectively on greens where a positive *hit* has to be made to reach the hole.

Most teaching professionals refuse to give their pupils more than rudimentary putting advice because, they say, putting is all a matter of personal preference. According to them, anything that feels right, probably is right. It is surprising that the most frustrating and exasperating area of the game is not more closely analysed by the individual golfer. Few weekend players ever stop to consider whether they are wrist putters, arm putters or a combination of the two. Yet how can they hope to produce an action that will not vary when they have failed to analyse this fundamental?

Casper is the greatest exponent of wrist putting: he gives the ball a sharp rap, with very little follow-through, that is supplied by the wrists with hardly any arm movement. Gary Player combines wrist and arm movement, perhaps the most popular of the three basic putting styles. But Bob Charles does all that is humanly possible to eliminate wrist action from his putting stroke, and the pendulum swing is made entirely with the arms and by rocking his shoulders.

This action is peculiarly suited to fast greens, but when faced with a long putt on a slow green, the length of the putting stroke is so great that it can lead to inaccuracies of striking. On such occasions, Charles uses a certain amount of wrist action to accelerate the clubhead through the ball.

Charles, who is almost six-feet-two in height, uses a very relaxed and upright stance, with no suggestion of hunching over the ball. This allows his arms to hang quite naturally from his shoulders. He positions the ball outside his left toe, so that the putter-blade makes contact slightly on the upswing which imparts the topspin that keeps the ball rolling towards the hole. His feet are square to the line.

Like most top professionals he uses the reverse overlap grip, with the index finger of his right hand overlapping the little finger of the left (remember he is left-handed). Thus, he has all the fingers of his left hand in contact with the shaft.

He makes the swing simply by rocking his shoulders, the hands and arms being almost completely passive. In other words, the triangle formed by his arms and shoulders moves as a complete unit. This not only keeps the putter blade low to the ground, but helps to keep it square to the hole throughout the stroke. Unlike the rap putters, who make a conscious effort to *strike* the back of the ball, Charles's pendulum swing tends to *push* the ball along the line, although he ensures that the clubhead is accelerating at the moment of contact.

Both the backswing and through-swing are appreciably longer than when wrist putting, and the only means of varying the length of the putt is by varying the length of the swing. The speed of the swing must not change, otherwise he risks an inaccurate strike.

Putter designs are legion, but because of his height and his upright posture, Charles uses a centre-shafted putter with an upright lie.

He has convinced me that his method is the once-and-for-all cure for the dreaded 'twitch', that fateful malady that imbues the hands with an involuntary life of their own, making it quite impossible for the player to take the club away from the ball on line without jerking it.

In the summer of 1972 I had been compelled to give up golf completely by this particular disease. Weeks of twitchy putting culminated on the 6th green at Deal in an air-putt, believe it or not! For once, I had been able to take the club back on line, but then instead of the hands jerking to left or right on the through-swing, they jumped vertically upwards towards my chin so that the putter cleared the top of the ball by a good four inches. It was more than flesh and blood could stand, and picking up my ball, I retired, hurt, to the clubhouse, vowing that I would play no more that year.

A few weeks later I was fortunate enough to see Charles win at both Turnberry and Newcastle, and made a particular study of his putting action. The most obvious difference was that I used a wrist action, while he eliminated the wrists from his swing. It then became clear that whatever causes the twitch, it is transmitted (in the case of a right-handed player) through the left wrist. If that wrist is allowed to collapse, or if it is overpowered by the right hand, the putter blade can obviously be jerked either to left or right. If there is no active participation by the hands or wrists, the whole torso would have to twitch to deflect the blade from its path.

At least, that was the theory, and while I maintained my vow not to play until 1973, many hours were spent carpet putting through the winter months, practising the 'Bob Charles Method' with one or two slight personal variations. When eventually tried on the golf course, the only great problem was to tailor the length of the swing to the length of the putt, but this became automatic after a couple of weeks.

I do not claim to be the best putter in the business as a result of this experiment, but if it gives the twitchers of the world any comfort, I have not twitched a putt since August 1972. It is still possible to mistime the stroke, or not to hit the ball in the blade's sweet-spot, and there has to be a conscious effort to push the blade right through towards the hole – but for me at least, Bob Charles has made the twitch a thing of the past. Yes, I know, what a thing to say. . . . It's really sticking one's chin out!

The professionals spend more time on the practice putting green than anywhere else. They develop a method that suits them, usually as simple a method as possible, and then they practise that method until it becomes second nature. Only by doing this do they give themselves the best possible chance of reproducing that stroke when the pressure is really on, and there is an Open Championship at stake.

Here is a lesson we can all learn. Find a method that is comfortable and seems to work, *then analyse it so that you know why it works*, and can see any ways in which it might be improved. Nothing gives more confidence on the greens than the knowledge of the reliability of your putting stroke. Then practise and practise.

Putting is not a matter of luck. People like Charles cannot get that lucky! It is as much a golf shot as the drive or the five-iron; on the scoreboard it has the same value, and needs to be studied and learned in just the same way.

43 Billy Casper is the master strategist for the ordinary golfer simply because he plays a game that is not based on power, but on reliability of technique and steadiness of results

CHAPTER THIRTEEN

The Champion Strategist: Billy Casper

It is strange to think that one of the finest golfers of our time has never been accepted by the general public as one of the game's super-stars, yet he has been accorded that accolade by his fellow professionals.

Had Billy Casper been a more outspoken man, he might well have insisted that the Big Three of the 1960s – Palmer, Player and Nicklaus – move over to make room for him and become the Big Four. His record speaks for itself: he joined the American Tour in 1956 as a rotund twenty-four-year-old. He won his first tournament in that year to presage one of the most remarkable sequences in the annals of sport. For the next sixteen years he was to win at least one US tournament every year, the pattern only being halted in 1972 when he had no victory to his credit. But in 1973 he won two more, and by the end of that year had fifty American tournament victories to his credit, and had earned only just short of a million and a half dollars in the United States. Only Nicklaus and Palmer had earned more at that time.

From 1958 until 1970 he had only twice been out of the first four in each year's money-winning lists, and he recorded the lowest scoring average in American golf five times between 1960 and 1968. In 1968 he became the first player in history to win more than $200,000 in one year on the US circuit.

Those statistics alone would place him among the all-time greats, but if further proof was needed, there were his two victories in the American Open, and one in the Masters.

Yet the golf-watching public never treated Casper with the awe they reserve for Nicklaus, the idolatry they keep for Palmer or the immense respect they have for Player. Why? possibly because Casper has been content to be just professional. He plays his golf with the minimum of fuss and frills, hides his personality behind a pleasant but unrevealing exterior, and makes no attempt at showmanship.

His fine putting, the most publicized part of his game, was accepted by many as his key to success, without giving any credit to the all-round excellence of his game. So Casper never captured the imagination of the public to the same degree as his more colourful rivals. Perhaps it was never quite so important to him.

Casper's game has no weaknesses, and no outstanding strength. He is a steady golfer, who rarely strays from the fairway, rarely fails to hit the greens in regulation figures, and shoots low rounds when the putts drop for him. What sets him apart from the other steady

44   One of golf's all-time greats, the mild-mannered Billy Casper

golfers on the American circuit is that he is one of the game's great thinkers. He tailors his game to the demands of the golf course without ever trying to stretch his shot-making ability beyond comfortable limits.

When Palmer and Nicklaus are trying to reach a par-five hole in two, they quite obviously pour extra physical power into the drive in order to reduce the length of the second shot. In the same situation, Casper steps up to the ball, takes his customary quick glance down the fairway, and then swings in just the same way as usual. Nor does he make any extra effort on the second shot. Yet the excellence of his short game yields as many birdies as his more aggressive colleagues.

There was one occasion, though, when resolutely sticking to his pre-tournament strategy cost Casper very dear, but he learnt his lesson, and had the opportunity to rectify the following year.

At famed Augusta in the Spring of 1969, Casper had decided to play the secure percentage game at which he excelled. It was a decision that was to cost him the Masters title. Augusta's par fives are notorious for their water hazards, and Casper contented himself with laying up short of these lakes in two, and then pitching to the flags. He made his pars throughout the tournament, but George Archer threw caution to the wind, and attacked them wherever he could. Consistently, Archer reached the par fives, which were well within Casper's range, and the birdies he earned won him the title with Casper second.

When he returned in 1970, Casper adopted a completely different strategy. Under tremendous pressure from Gene Littler on the last day, he attacked all the long holes and made his birdies. He hit iron shots straight at the flag, no matter what the perils that lay between him and his target. At the 17th and 18th holes, he had two very possible birdie putts, either of which would have won the title outright. He hit both boldly at the back of the hole; they hit the cup and stayed out.

This was no conservative percentage golfer. This was a great player gambling everything to win one of the world's great golfing titles. He carried the same mood through into the play-off round the following day, still firing straight at the flag – even when he was far ahead of poor Littler.

Surely the most remarkable day's golf in modern golfing history also featured Billy Casper. After three and a half rounds of the 1966 US Open, played at the Olympic Club, San Francisco, Arnold Palmer was moving smoothly towards the title. This was a great day for him, the possibility of his first major championship since the 1964 Masters; and this would silence the critics who maintained that 'Palmer is over the hill'.

Arnie's Army was going mad. He had led by three strokes from Casper at the start of the round, but with a sensational outward nine of 32, had now drawn no less than seven strokes clear of the 1959 winner. All he had to do was cruise the rest of the way to the vast acclaim of his fans.

That was the psychological mistake he made, as he admitted afterwards. For now, instead of the aggressive Palmer booming his driver from the tee, he became a man just trying to keep the ball in play on the tree-lined fairways. For most of the back nine he used a one-iron from the tee, and if club golfers feel that they are the only ones who try to steer the ball with disastrous results when there is a cup at stake, they should have seen Palmer in San Francisco.

Palmer's visits to the trees became more frequent and Casper needed no second bidding. Instead of plugging steadily along to collect second prize, he changed his strategy completely in mid-round, and aimed at the flag on every possible occasion. His courage was rewarded, and the putts kept dropping. After eight holes, he

*45 and 46   Casper demonstrating a pitch-and-run shot with a seven-iron. Note
how the hands lead the clubhead into the ball*

had made up the seven-stroke leeway, covering the back nine in 31, and had forced a tie.

In the play-off the following day, Palmer led by two strokes after nine holes, but when Casper holed from nearly twenty yards at the 13th, the tide turned dramatically. With the memory of his collapse still all too clear, Palmer repeated his errors, allowing Casper to win by four shots – 69 to 73. Sadly for Arnold, this was the third time in five years that he had lost a play-off for the title, and record books show that his only victory in this event was back in 1960.

There are two important lessons to be learned from that event. The first is that no golfer can afford to change his natural pattern of play. When the attacking Palmer became defensive he lost momentum, and the adrenalin that had carried him to a seven-stroke lead drained away. The second lesson is that every golfer should be ready to seize any opportunity that may come along, *but* only if the golfer is still playing within his capabilities. Casper played the last nine holes at Olympic in a totally contrasting style to his previous three and a half rounds. He had his fair share of luck; but he never asked more of his shot-making than he knew was possible.

This is the key to Casper's tournament strategy, and it should be the underlying factor in every golfer's thinking. When the pressure is on, when the Captain's Prize is in sight, no one can expect to hit shots that he knows perfectly well he cannot achieve when he is completely relaxed and playing for fun.

Like all today's champions, Casper carries a mental chart of every hole. Unlike the Nicklauses and the Weiskopf's, he does not believe in pacing off yardages, but relies on the judgement of his eyes when estimating distance. However, Casper's mental plan takes in the entire shape and form of each hole, so that before he reaches the tee he has a clear idea of which side of the fairway the drive has to be hit in order to give him the easiest approach to the green, and at which part of the green he should aim to leave himself the simplest putt.

The majority of handicap golfers may well think only in terms of leaving their drives on the fairway, and getting on to any part of the putting green, but at championship level, such golf would bring few rewards. And even the club golfer would stand to improve his scoring considerably if he would only think of a hole in its entirety, and then play that hole within his limitations.

Unfortunately, a great many *handicap* players seem to feel that they should score par at every hole, and as a result, try to do the impossible. What is so wrong with intentionally playing a troublesome par four as a par five in order to protect a good score, when to attempt reaching the green in two could lead to a seven or worse?

No one wants to make weekend club golf the tedious, slow affair that so much professional tournament golf has become. But if a man is to play within his limitations, he must know what those limitations are. How many amateurs, for instance, have paced out on the practice ground the maximum distances they can expect with each club, when reasonably struck?

Champions do as much as possible to eliminate guesswork from their golf. Yet the club player is guessing most of the time. He must surely be able to lop off one or two shots from his scores if he knows what he can reasonably expect from every club in the bag, and if he knows the distances of the second shots from certain fixed points around his own golf course.

Casper is the model strategist for the ordinary golfer simply because he plays a game that is not based on power, but on reliability of technique and steadiness of results. He is also a model for those who believe that golf has to be played at an interminably slow pace. Among the professionals, nobody completes a shot with such alacrity – no matter how great the pressure or the importance of the stroke. He seems barely to give any thought to a shot, but that is not so. He has done his thinking in advance.

Spectators at British tournaments have never had the opportunity of seeing this reserved and self-effacing Mormon at his best, for although his style would seem to suit the best of our championship courses, he has never featured particularly strongly in a major event on this side of the Atlantic.

Perhaps his best years are behind him now, for although his method will endure for as long as he cares to compete, it is possible that some of the drive, without which no man can scale the dizziest heights, is lacking.

But if Nicklaus is the greatest golfer of the modern era – and with a record number of major championship wins to his credit he must be considered so – then, in my opinion, Casper has filled the runner-up spot. Despite the fact that nearly all his successes have been in America, he has maintained an extraordinarily high standard over nearly two decades without threatening to burn himself out. He has done it all by thoughtfully planning his way round the golf course, never attempting to stretch beyond his limits.

CHAPTER FOURTEEN

A Champion's Temperament: Ben Hogan

Many years ago, Arnold Palmer was quoted as saying: 'Golf is 5 per cent physical and 95 per cent mental.' Many golfers would perhaps argue a little over his proportions, since few would claim Palmer's physical ability to hit a golf ball. But at his level he was undoubtedly correct. The champions have a golf game ingrained into their systems, usually since childhood, and this is sharpened by countless hundreds of hours on the practice ground.

So when it comes down to winning The Big One, whatever championship it may be, the strain is not on technique, but on temperament.

If all today's great players had come out of the same temperamental mould they would be dull company indeed. In fact, as individuals, they are as different as any large cross-section of the population. Trevino bubbles his extrovert way towards the next million dollars, while Casper acquires his wealth in unassuming fashion; Player constantly frets about his swing and is prepared to take advice from anybody who stands on the practice ground long enough; Nicklaus works on his game in a perpetual state of crowded isolation.

Yet no matter what the outward signs, when these four men step on to the first tee in one of the major championships, there is the same core running through each of them. In their separate ways they have brought themselves to concert pitch, a state of mental and physical readiness for the big test. Now they are just totally dedicated to producing their best, almost more for their own self-satisfaction than for the title or the money. They know they are the best in the world, but they have to go on proving this to themselves.

Perhaps the fact was never better demonstrated than by the forbidding figure of Ben Hogan, who in terms of sheer striking ability, was almost certainly the greatest.

In 1948 Hogan, then thirty-six, had arrived at the pinnacle of his career. He won the US Open and PGA Championship that year, and there was nobody who could approach his mastery from tee to green. In 1946 he had won the colossal amount of over $42,000, an unheard-of sum for a golfer to collect in one year, and in 1948 he again headed the money winners with over $32,000. All the years of struggling in pro golf, living on fruit and little else, were beginning to pay off.

Then on his way home from a tournament on a foggy Texas night in 1949, Hogan's car was in a head-on collision with a bus. So bad were his leg injuries that the doctors gave him little chance of walking, and absolutely none of playing golf again. Only he and his wife will ever really know what it took to win the fight back to the top, but unbelievably he won the 1950 US Open. Suffering pain and exhaustion, he tied with Lloyd Mangrum and George Fazio and shot 69 in the play-off to take the title easily.

Far from destroying a brilliant career, Hogan's terrible injuries seemed to create in him a firmer resolve to prove himself the best. The vintage years still lay ahead.

In 1951 he retained the US Open at Oakland Hills, Michigan, and won his first Masters title at Augusta. When he won both events again, in 1953, he decided it was time to aim at what he considered the third leg of the modern Grand Slam – the Open Championship in Britain. At that time, the US PGA title was not as revered as it is today.

The whole world knew that Hogan was invincible in 1953 when he crossed the Atlantic for his one and only attempt at the world's oldest championship. At Augusta he had totalled 274 to win by five strokes from Ed Oliver, and his score was also five strokes inside the record for the event, set by Ralph Guldahl in 1939. Hogan's total was to stand until Jack Nicklaus's incredible winning score of 271 in 1965. At Oakmont Hogan had deprived Sam Snead of his chance to win his first US Open. Hogan led by two shots at the halfway stage, and from then on, Snead faltered under the pressure. The Iron Man's winning total was 283, and no less convincing than his victory at the Masters.

America, and Britain too, lauded the greatest professional of them all. His clinical approach and icy temperament did not endear him to the galleries in the way Arnold Palmer is loved by his fans, but those who watched Hogan knew they were watching a man do something better than anyone had ever done it before.

No one is more critical of golf than the knowledgeable Scottish spectators, and as they clamoured to watch Hogan play his practice rounds over a Carnoustie stretched to 7,200 yards, they soon appreciated that he had an odds-on chance of winning the Open Championship.

In every practice round Hogan played three balls off each tee – one down the centre, one down the left, and one down the right. Then he played each iron shot to the green. By the time he had finished his preparations, he knew just about every blade of grass on the course. The links did not please him, and he said so. The Scots can be as brusque as Hogan, and replied that a real champion could adjust himself to any conditions.

Hogan produced a 73 in the first round of the Championship, and refused to be interviewed by the press. Frank Stranahan, a wealthy American amateur who was to turn professional shortly afterwards, took the lead with a 70. The home crowd had roared Eric Brown on to a 71, then came Peter Thomson, Dai Rees and Roberto de Vicenzo all on 72.

Hogan had the same effect on competitors and spectators that Nicklaus has today. By his very presence, he could psyche everybody else out of this championship, and already they were looking over their shoulders, wondering when he would make his move.

At the halfway stage, the loyalties of the Scots were sharply divided, for while they respected the 'wee ice mon', as they had christened Hogan, as being the best in the world, it was Eric Brown who had taken over the lead with another 71, along with Rees, whose 70 was the best of the tournament so far. De Vicenzo was a shot behind at 143, with Stranahan, Thomson and Hogan at 144.

Inexorably, Hogan took over the lead after 54 holes, his 70 being the most precise golfing skill that Carnoustie had so far seen. But perhaps to his surprise, he had not yet shaken off the opposition. De Vicenzo recorded his second consecutive 71 to tie with him at 214, while Thomson, Rees and another Argentinian professional, Antonio Cerda, were only a stroke behind. Cerda had made his challenge with the first sub-70 round of the Championship.

Hogan took a solitary lunch, then headed silently for the practice ground, followed by half the population of Scotland.

What happened that afternoon is now in the history books. Stranahan came bursting back up the field with a 69, Rees, Thomson and Cerda never wilted and produced 71s apiece – they all tied at 286. De Vicenzo took 73 to finish at 287, and he waited another fourteen years before the Championship jug became his.

But Hogan was playing a different brand of golf. He had been totally prepared for this championship, and had come all this way to win. Now was the time to prove the point. The superiority of his play over those who vainly chased him was plain for all to see. His 68 and four-stroke winning margin was no more than justice being seen to be done.

Golf writers and public alike went wild with praise over the wee ice mon. Hogan had no chink in his armour, and no chink in his ice-cold temperament. He was the only man who appeared unmoved by what he had done at Carnoustie that day. He left the little Angus town as he had arrived a fortnight before – without a smile, but with the Open Championship trophy tucked away in his trunk.

Although in his sixties now, Hogan still makes the occasional appearance in a major American tournament, and almost invariably finishes in the top ten. In 1967 he produced a 66, the lowest single round of the Masters that year, in his third round. Even the best of the current crop of super-stars will readily admit that even now Hogan is still the game's greatest striker. A putting twitch finally put paid to his career. In his latter years as a tournament regular, it was pathetic to see the hands tighten on the putter grip, and Hogan's inability to take the blade smoothly back from the ball.

They called him the Iron Man, and he lived up to that reputation both on and off the golf course. Years of privation and dedication as he struggled towards the pinnacle left their mark on his character. When they are on the course, today's champions must possess the same iron will to win, and the same facility to cut themselves off in a world of concentration.

We may find it remarkable that Trevino can be engaged in playful banter with the crowds one moment, then able to switch himself off and immerse himself in this state of utter concentration the next, but it is so. Trevino, in fact, openly admits that his playing to the crowd is merely a useful safety valve for the pent-up tension that tournament play imposes.

Any player that reaches the top in these cut-throat days has only arrived there through a combination of dedication, hard work, imagination and a streak of killer instinct. For Hogan, Nicklaus, Player, Weiskopf, Miller and the rest, golf is more than a living, more than a sport. It is their way of impressing their superiority on those around them. If they had entered the field of commerce, without ever touching a golf club, they could well have become millionaires anyway. Golf at the highest level has moulded their temperaments and personalities, but the raw material was always there.

This discipline, this refusal to acquiesce to pressure, sets the champions apart from the many professionals who are physically equipped just as efficiently, and have comparable stroke-making ability, but somehow never quite break through to the top.

CHAPTER FIFTEEN

Towards the Club Championship

Were it possible to become a top-class golfer by reading books there would be no rabbits.

I can guarantee that no one who has read this far will become a super-star as a result of what they have read. On the other hand, by studying the champions, you can learn important lessons that can greatly improve performance on your own golf course.

No one can learn a champion's shot-making technique, because every man's swing is as individual as his fingerprint. Only your own teacher can help you to arrive at a swing exactly tailored to your age, physical condition and aptitude – a swing that works for *you*. A course of lessons is the best investment that any club golfer can ever make, for a professional can save time and heartache by putting his finger immediately on your basic problems. It is odd how often a handicap golfer who tries to sort out his own problems completely misses the root cause of his troubles and starts messing about unnecessarily with parts of his swing that need no attention.

The weekend player can learn from watching the stars and studying their thinking – the most powerful weapon in the bag. The amateur will see shots that he might never have attempted in the normal course of his play, like the push-shot to the green through the wind. It is well worth spending a little time on the practice ground experimenting with these special shots. They can become stroke-savers at the crucial moment.

Another factor common to the best players, and yet so often over-looked by club golfers is that they always play the easiest possible shot, the one with the greatest percentage chance of success. All too often the weekend golfer attempts a delicate cut-up wedge shot, when a seven-iron pitch-and-run stands a better chance of finishing near the hole and is a lot less difficult to play.

Remember when you watch the champions at work that they achieved their mastery through many hours of practice. No weekend golfer, with limited time to spend at the club, wants his game to be drudgery, but then I have never yet met a golfer of any standard who did not want to play better than he does. The answer is in his own hands.

Even a few minutes of regular thoughtful practice will bring rewards, particularly if the practice concentrates on and around the greens. This is where the greatest number of shots are saved, and where champions devote the vast majority of their practice time.

The practice ground is where any golfer can find his best natural rhythm. When studying the methods of the champions in these pages, the word 'tempo' constantly recurred. Tempo, or thythm, is as individual as the swing itself. Here is the vital factor that makes the swing work at peak efficiency.

If you can find your natural rhythm, and find also some mental gimmick that helps you to retain it when you are playing, you will be much less susceptible to the pressures of competition.

Perhaps most important of all was the lesson to be learned from Billy Casper, who carries an image in his mind's eye of the best way to play each hole, pictures each shot he has to play and never attempts a shot that is obviously beyond his capabilities.

Golfers are supreme optimists and like to believe that they are capable of the impossible. Deep down, however, every golfer knows what he can and what he cannot reasonably do. If he is honest with himself – and golf is the ultimate form of self-analysis – he knows how far his capabilities extend.

I trust that as a result of my labours and reflections on great moments of golfing history, those capabilities may be extended a little further.

You may never win the Open Championship, but perhaps you are a little nearer to winning your Club Championship.